THE JUSTICE BELL

The Woman's Liberty Bell

Silent Until November 2nd

1776
LIBERTY

1915
EQUALITY

"LIBERTY THROUGHOUT THE LAND TO ALL THE INHABITANTS THEREOF"
Was the Message of

THE LIBERTY BELL OF 1776

It proclaimed the birth of a new nation "DEDICATED TO THE PROPOSITION THAT JUST GOVERNMENTS DERIVE THEIR POWER FROM THE CONSENT OF THE GOVERNED" AND THAT "TAXATION WITHOUT REPRESENTATION IS TYRANNY."

Today, fifty million of these inhabitants are women, but only four million of them have received the full benefits of the Liberty which the old bell proclaimed. These four million women live in the equal suffrage states of the West and Middle West. The people of these states think as did Abraham Lincoln who said:

"I GO FOR ALL SHARING THE PRIVILEGES OF GOVERNMENT WHO ASSIST IN BEARING ITS BURDENS, BY NO MEANS EXCLUDING WOMEN"

Even as the original Liberty Bell rang first for Pennsylvania in 1776 so should the new Liberty Bell proclaim a new message of Liberty first in Pennsylvania this year. The new bell is the Woman's Liberty Bell, which is to ring for the first time on the day that the Women of Pennsylvania are granted the right to vote. Every fair-minded man in Pennsylvania will help to make this day November second next

Because every fairminded man believes in Justice and
Because Justiee is an empty word so long as half the population of a Commonwealth have no say in the making of its laws.
The Liberty Bell of 1776 rang to "proclaim Liberty" to create our nation.
The Woman's Liberty Bell will ring to "establish justice"—to compiete our nation.

Help break the chains that hold the bronze clapper silent.
Vote "Yes" on the Suffrage Amendment on Election Day.

Pennsylvania Woman Suffrage Association
Campaign Headquarters:—201 Arcade Building, Harrisburg, Pennsylvania

Pennsylvania Woman Suffrage Association flyer promoting the women's suffrage amendment on Election Day, November 2, 1915.

THE JUSTICE BELL

TRACING THE JOURNEY OF A FORGOTTEN SYMBOL

Amanda Owen

Justice Bell Foundation

Printed in the United States of America

First Printing, 2025

ISBN: 978-0-9848209-1-7

Cover design by Jeff Witchel and Amanda Owen
Book design by Amanda Owen

Justice Bell Foundation
700 Ardmore Avenue, Unit 125
Ardmore, PA 19003
www.justicebell.org

This book is dedicated to those who fight for equality and stand up to injustice. May their determination be a lesson in the power of never giving up.

History isn't what happened. It's who tells the story.
—Sally Roesch Wagner

Contents

PART THREE
After the Tour

PART FOUR
What Happened tothe Justice Bell?

Preface

In 1915, a one-ton bronze bell traveled across Pennsylvania, its clapper chained and muted to symbolize the silencing of women's voices. Shepherded by a determined band of suffragists, the Justice Bell became a rallying cry for equality and a call for men to vote for a referendum that would grant the women of the state the right to vote. This impressive symbol drew thousands of people to hear speeches at roadside gatherings and in small towns, and it attracted even larger crowds in big cities, where they could see the bell and participate in suffrage parades. Yet today, the story of the bell and of the tenacious women who championed it remains largely forgotten.

My fascination with the Justice Bell began in 2015, when I came across a brief online reference to it while researching the women's suffrage movement. I was astonished to learn that the bell had once been a national symbol for voting rights. Between 1915 and 1920, more than a million people had seen it, and updates on its journey appeared in newspapers across the country. The Justice Bell was an exact replica of the Liberty Bell except for two details: it wasn't cracked and, in addition to the words on the Liberty Bell, "Proclaim Liberty Throughout All the Land Unto All the Inhabitants thereof," it bore an inscription from the Preamble to the United States Constitution: *Establish Justice*. It rang for the first time after the ratification of the Nineteenth Amendment, during a celebration attended by ten thousand people on September 25, 1920, in Philadelphia's Independence Square.

What happened to the bell after 1920? I could not find anyone who had ever heard of it—including librarians, teachers, and women's rights leaders. When I asked, "Have you ever heard of the Justice Bell?" the answer was always the same: "What bell?"

My search eventually led me to the Washington Memorial Chapel, a small privately owned church in the middle of Pennsylvania's Valley Forge National

Historical Park, where I found the Justice Bell in the rotunda of the chapel's bell tower. When I asked a woman working there if she had any literature about the Justice Bell, she looked puzzled and replied, "What bell?" She knew nothing about it. The lack of awareness, even among those working beside the bell, sparked a years-long journey through archives and newspapers to uncover the story of the once-famous Justice Bell and the clever women who used it as a symbol of the fight for voting rights.

I began by tracking down descendants of suffragists who had traveled with the Justice Bell, and I located the chapel's retired rector, who, in the early 1990s, had rescued the bell from the woods where it had been abandoned. I enlisted archivists and volunteers at historical societies and museums across Pennsylvania to help me sift through microfilm and undigitized newspapers in an effort to map the bell's path during its historic tour.

Through my research into the lives of these suffragists, I found that many accounts defied traditional depictions of women from this era as primarily devoted to home and family life. They were feisty and resourceful. They came from diverse backgrounds and contributed to the movement in myriad ways. College students and other young people sought to build a more just society. Affluent women financed the movement while actively organizing and campaigning. Black women saw the vote as a vital tool in the fight against racial inequality, and working women championed labor reforms, including better working conditions and restrictions on child labor. In the pages that follow, you will meet many of these remarkable women.

This book represents the first in-depth documentation of the Justice Bell's creation, historic tour, years of obscurity, and rediscovery. It does not provide a comprehensive history of the women's suffrage movement but, rather, details one story among many that took place during this pivotal period of activism.

I wrote *The Justice Bell* to ensure that this chapter in American history becomes part of the historical record. But the journey of the bell and the women who used it to bring attention to their campaign for the vote is not just a story about the past. Its message remains relevant, offering lessons in tactics and the importance of persistence. Grassroots campaigns require deep dedication. We stand on the shoulders of those who came before us, and knowing who they are and what they did matters.

The Justice Bell is presented in four parts. Part One provides an overview of American women's voting rights in the late nineteenth and early twentieth centuries, focusing on Pennsylvania, where earlier efforts paved the way for the bell's journey. Part Two follows the bell's 1915 tour, featuring highlights from its travels, biographies of the suffragists who campaigned alongside it, and newspaper articles that capture the spirit of the campaign. Lightly edited for clarity, these articles serve as both a record of the journey and a resource for further research. Part Three traces the bell's role from the 1915 campaign to the ratification of the Nineteenth Amendment in 1920. Part Four examines the bell's fall into obscurity and the efforts to secure its place in the historical record. The afterword reports on ongoing initiatives to preserve the memory of the Justice Bell, ensuring its legacy endures. These efforts underscore the critical importance of safeguarding women's stories and their role in shaping history.

More than a century after the women's suffrage movement, the themes represented by the Justice Bell still resonate in today's ongoing pursuit of equality. By sharing its story, I hope to inspire readers to explore the contributions women have made to our nation's history and recognize the roles they continue to play, ensuring their voices become part of the ever-evolving story of America.

Introduction

Reverend Richard Lyon Stinson arrived as a new rector at the Washington Memorial Chapel in January 1992. This was an ideal assignment for an Episcopalian minister who was also a history buff. The chapel, built in 1903 to honor George Washington, sits on private land within Valley Forge National Historical Park in Pennsylvania, occupying the location where Washington's Continental Army encamped during the brutal winter of 1777–78.

As Rev. Stinson surveyed the grounds and the adjacent woods, he came upon an enormous bronze bell surrounded by chicken wire and with a small roof over it. The bell was in obvious disrepair, and he wondered what it was doing there. It looked like the famous Liberty Bell, but upon closer examination, he saw it was engraved with the words "Establish Justice." So, not a Liberty Bell replica. What was it? He asked the staff at the chapel and learned that the bell was an artifact from the women's suffrage movement and was called the Justice Bell. But why was it here? He wanted to know more.

He rummaged in the basement and found information about the chapel's founding rector, Reverend W. Herbert Burk, and discovered he had collected numerous historical objects with a goal of creating a center of American culture that would include several museums. He surmised that Rev. Burk must have persuaded the suffragists to give the bell to the chapel.

Rev. Stinson's mother had been a member of the League of Women Voters, an organization he knew to be the continuation of the National American Woman Suffrage Association (NAWSA). Wanting to reunite the bell with its organization, he called the League's Pennsylvania office, located at that time in Philadelphia, and spoke to Sara "Sallie" Corbishley.

"I have your bell!" he said.

"What bell?" she asked.

Until Rev. Stinson's call, League members had been unaware of the bell's existence. Corbishley had a vague memory of seeing stacks of old glass-plate negatives that had images of a bell, ten years prior to this phone call. They had been stashed in paper grocery bags at the League's state headquarters. After the call from Rev. Stinson, she wondered if the bell found in the woods was the one in the photographs.

Indeed, it was. And with that phone call, history was retrieved from paper bags filled with photographs that chronicled one of the most dramatic chapters of the women's suffrage movement.

PART ONE

A Brief History

VOTES FOR WOMEN A SUCCESS

THE MAP PROVES IT

WOMEN VOTE IN ALL THE WHITE STATES WHY NOT IN THIS STATE?

The Vote was given to Women in

Wyoming	1869	Arizona	1912
Colorado	1893	Kansas	1912
Idaho	1896	Oregon	1912
Utah	1896	Alaska	1913
Washington	1910	Montana	1914
California	1911	Nevada	1914

Nearly 4,000,000 women vote in the Equal Suffrage States.
Total Number of Electoral Votes in Equal Suffrage States—91.

VOTE FOR WOMAN SUFFRAGE

GIVE THIS TO A FRIEND AND ASK HIM TO VOTE FOR IT

PENNSYLVANIA WOMAN SUFFRAGE ASSOCIATION
Headquarters: 201-5 Arcade Building, Harrisburg 142

N. W. S. Publishing Co., Inc.

Map highlighting the state-by-state campaign for women's voting rights, National American Woman Suffrage Association, 1915.

The State-by-State Effort

Convincing men to grant women the right to vote was a daunting task. Although suffragists had to be (and were) persistent, men had placed themselves in all positions of leadership and were unwilling to share power. The one fleeting exception came in 1776, with New Jersey's first state constitution, which used language implying that women who owned property were allowed to vote.[1] In 1790, a new state voting law included the words "he or she," thereby explicitly enfranchising women who owned property. But in November 1807, the all-male legislature amended the constitution to officially deny voting rights to anyone who was not a White male taxpayer.[2] Sixty-two years would pass before American women had voting rights again.

In 1869, the men in the Wyoming Territory granted women the right to vote. The Utah Territory followed in 1870, and the Washington Territory in 1883.

When Wyoming became a state in 1890, it retained women's suffrage, becoming the first state to enfranchise women, following New Jersey's brief experiment a century earlier. Over the next two decades, other states joined the movement: Colorado (1893), Idaho and Utah (1896), Washington (1910), California (1911), Arizona, Kansas, and Oregon (1912), and the Alaska Territory (1913). Men in several additional states granted partial suffrage, allowing women to vote in limited capacities, such as in municipal elections.

In Pennsylvania, where the Pennsylvania Woman Suffrage Association (PWSA) was founded in 1869 with the express goal of securing the ballot, the men in power refused to budge. With neither full nor partial suffrage, Pennsylvania women could not vote on anything—not even for local school board positions.

The PWSA gained momentum in 1910 when it opened its headquarters in Philadelphia, the association's first physical location. Two years later, during the November 1912 state convention, Pittsburgh suffragists were elected to leadership positions for the first time: Jennie Bradley Roessing became president, Mary Bakewell was named western region vice president, Lucy Kennedy Miller took on the role of corresponding secretary, and Hannah Patterson served as auditor. That same year, the PWSA relocated its headquarters from Philadelphia to Harrisburg, the state capital.

To oversee the organization's work, Roessing and Patterson moved to Harrisburg, where the new offices in the Arcade Building, just one block from the state capitol, provided easy access to legislators. Roessing later reported, "An executive secretary was installed, and Miss Patterson and I supervised the work, living in Harrisburg for most of these three years [1913–1915]. We were literally on the job day and night, for the work grew, and at no time did we have the money for the help needed. So, besides the field work, which we both did, there was always the office work."[3]

Before the Pittsburgh women took charge, suffragists from the eastern part of the state, particularly in Philadelphia and its surrounding counties, largely framed women's suffrage as an issue of justice and fairness. They relied on educational strategies by conducting meetings and distributing literature. The Pittsburgh suffragists believed it was essential to highlight the practical reasons for women's suffrage—what we now call kitchen table issues. They also understood the importance of convincing state representatives to support their goal. Although the PWSA had not been successful in getting a suffrage amendment passed by the legislature in 1911, they had since become more organized and were ready to try again.

In anticipation of the 1913 legislative session, the PWSA launched a strategic campaign later known as the Pittsburgh Plan. The initiative involved appointing suffragists to counties and districts where they would tailor their approach to the specific needs of each community and report back to a central command. The PWSA also established local men's leagues in support of women's suffrage and held classes to train women in writing and delivering compelling speeches. It was a boots-on-the-ground effort that reached every corner of the state.

Their efforts paid off when the state House of Representatives voted in favor of the amendment, 131 to 70, on February 5, 1913, and the state Senate followed on April 22, passing it by a vote of 26 to 22. The following day, Roessing expressed her joy in an interview with the *Pittsburgh Post*:

> "Our satisfaction is too great to be expressed in mere words, and we cannot find phrases sufficiently strong to thank the friends who have stood by us loyally through this trying campaign. The fight in the future will be waged along the same lines as in the past, and we have not the slightest doubt that when the people vote on the question in 1915, they will amend the Constitution so that both men and women can vote in Pennsylvania."[4]

In Pennsylvania, the state legislature must pass a proposed amendment in two successive terms by a majority in both houses for it to be placed on the ballot for voters to decide.

Over the next two years, the suffragists increased their lobbying efforts in hopes of winning over more state senators and representatives, and they traveled throughout the state to gain greater public support for the amendment. During that time, Roessing's health suffered from the strain of the round-the-clock work, and Patterson stepped in as acting president of the PWSA from February until November of 1914.[5]

SUFFRAGIST SPOTLIGHT

Jennie Bradley Roessing (1881–1963)

Jennie Bradley Roessing, November 7, 915.

Jennie Bradley Roessing, the only child of John Bradley and Anna Marie Friedrich Bradley, was born on May 11, 1881, in Pittsburgh, where her father owned a custom tailoring business. In 1904, at age twenty-three, she and Hannah Patterson, Mary Flinn, Lucy Kennedy, and Mary Bakewell founded the Allegheny County Equal Rights Association (ACERA), which was renamed the Equal Franchise Federation of Western Pennsylvania in 1910. She married Frank Myler Roessing on September 21, 1908, after which she was known as Mrs. Frank M. Roessing. The couple had no children and later divorced.[6]

Elected president of the Pennsylvania Woman Suffrage Association (PWSA) in 1912, Roessing became an effective leader of the state's suffrage movement. She worked especially closely with Hannah Patterson as they lobbied legislators and traveled throughout the state between 1913 and 1915 to support local organizers and deliver speeches advocating for women's suffrage. Their deep friendship and mutual respect lasted a lifetime.

As PWSA president, Roessing oversaw all aspects of the 1915 Votes for Women campaign, which included the Justice Bell tour. She accompanied the bell during part of its journey, sometimes driving the truck that carried it.

In November 1915, Roessing was elected first vice president of the National American Woman Suffrage Association (NAWSA) and began spending much of her time in Washington, DC. She returned to Pittsburgh in 1917 to care for her ailing father, but remained active in social and civic affairs. She helped establish recreational centers for children and played a key role in creating Allegheny County's first independent juvenile court.[7]

In 1935, she considered running for Congress but abandoned the idea after a poll suggested that Pennsylvania voters were unwilling to elect a woman. Four years later, she helped organize a campaign to elect Judge Sara M. Soffel to the Pennsylvania Supreme Court, although Soffel was not successful. In 1941, Roessing managed Soffel's campaign for a seat on the Allegheny County Common Pleas Court, which Soffel won. Roessing remained active in civic affairs in Pittsburgh until her death on May 15, 1963, at the age of eighty-two.[8]

Creating a Woman's Liberty Bell

While the all-out effort to get an amendment on the ballot proceeded, Katharine Wentworth Ruschenberger (Mrs. Charles Wister Ruschenberger) of Strafford, Chester County, developed a plan to create a replica of the Liberty Bell. She believed that suffragists should have their own symbol to rally behind: a Woman's Liberty Bell. A dedicated suffragist and a woman of means, she was willing to cover the $2,000 cost of the bell (approximately $62,000 in 2025) and an additional $2,000 for a White Motor Company car to carry the bell. A civil engineer from Strafford, W. Lowndes Browning, would convert the vehicle into an auto truck with a flatbed for the two-thousand-pound bronze bell and a rear platform where suffragists could deliver speeches at public gatherings. Later, newspapers would refer to it as either an auto truck or the bell truck.[9]

In 1913, with the enthusiastic support from the PWSA board, Ruschenberger commissioned the Meneely Bell Company in Troy, New York, to create a replica of the Liberty Bell with only two design changes: It would have no crack, and above the inscription "Proclaim Liberty Throughout All the Land Unto All the Inhabitants thereof," it would bear the words "Establish Justice," taken from the Preamble to the United States Constitution. She also requested that the bell's clapper be chained, rendering it mute until women could vote.

While she waited for the foundry to complete its work, Ruschenberger had a large plaster bell constructed that could be used until the bronze one was ready. She advertised this version in the same way she would later promote the real bell, calling it both the Woman's Liberty Bell and the Justice Bell. Even though it was made of plaster, she made sure to let people know that its clapper was chained to symbolize the silencing of women's voices.

This plaster bell was featured in three significant parades in 1913: the national suffrage parade on March 3 in Washington, DC; the women's suffrage parade that was part of the Perry Centennial celebration in Erie, Pennsylvania, on July 8; and a parade in Brooklyn, New York, on November 1.

Liberty Bell's Message

The Liberty Bell float probably will be introduced at this point, constituting a prologue to the several divisions of the parade. The float will carry an exact replica of old Liberty Bell suspended above the tree tops and the people and the float will bear on a banner the words, "We claim the Bell's last message, Justice."

The underlying idea of the Liberty Bell float, which is sent from the Pennsylvania Woman Suffrage Association by Katherine Wentworth Rushenberger, is that Liberty Bell has two messages—Liberty and Justice. The Pennsylvania women describe the idea of the float thus:

"Liberty Bell's first message is liberty, July 8, 1776, it rang to proclaim liberty throughout the land and unto all inhabitants thereof. Yet the Nation was organized giving self-government to men only. For this reason came the imperative necessity of a second message. The second message is Justice. July 8, 1835, while tolling for the death of John Marshall, Chief Justice of the United States, Liberty Bell cracked into eternal silence, proclaiming thus its final message that Liberty cannot survive Justice."

The plaster Justice Bell made its debut in the national women's suffrage parade in Washington, DC, March 3, 1913.

The plaster Justice Bell displayed on a parade float during the Perry Centennial celebrations in Erie, Pennsylvania, July 8, 1913.

THE LIBERTY BELL FLOAT, A STRIKING FEATURE OF THE PARADE.

The plaster Justice Bell on a float in a women's suffrage parade in Brooklyn, New York, November 1, 1913.

The Pennsylvania Woman Suffrage Association convention attendees in front of the Hotel Casey, Scranton, Pennsylvania, November 1914.

The following year, the plaster bell made a prominent appearance at the 46th annual convention of the PWSA, held at the Hotel Casey in Scranton from November 19 to 24, 1914. The bell was dramatically displayed in the rotunda of the hotel as more than three hundred women gathered to attend workshops and planning sessions for the upcoming 1915 Votes for Women campaign. Ruschenberger was scheduled to give a talk titled "The New Liberty Bell" on the morning of November 24, but due to a bad cold, she was unable to attend.[10]

Louise Hall, a popular speaker and organizing secretary for the PWSA, volunteered to serve as director of the Justice Bell tour. Her brother, Oliver Hall, a recent MIT graduate, signed on as the driver.

Louise Hall (1881–1966)

Louise Hall, ca. 1915

Annie Louise Hall was born on January 15, 1881, in Pensacola, Florida, the daughter of a naval officer, Martin Ellsworth Hall, and Mary Cushing Hall. She was raised in Lowell, Massachusetts, with her three siblings.

Thirty-four-year-old Louise Hall was already a veteran of the movement when she became director of the Justice Bell tour and one of its most popular speakers. A 1903 graduate of Vassar College, she taught at private girls' schools before moving to

New York City to work in the settlement houses, where she was radicalized through her contact with women and children living in poverty. In 1910, she became active in suffrage work in Massachusetts, and by 1912, she was organizing in Rhode Island and Ohio.[11] The PWSA hired her in 1913 as its full-time executive secretary and, a year later, as organizing secretary. Hall traveled with the Justice Bell tour from its launch in Sayre, Pennsylvania, on June 23, 1915, until October 12, when she was dispatched from Lebanon County to Philadelphia and then to several other locations to assist with last-minute campaigning ahead of the November 2 election.[12]

She was described in multiple newspapers as an especially gifted speaker. One account from July 29, 1915, called her "one of the best suffrage campaign speakers in the country." It continued: "Her introductory speeches make the justice of the suffrage cause so clear that the message of the chained and silent bell arouses an irresistible determination in the audiences to see that the women of Pennsylvania get the justice of enfranchisement and are enabled to unchain their Bell and proclaim that fact."[13]

After the Pennsylvania campaign, Hall continued her suffrage work, organizing in New York, Connecticut, and New Hampshire. In 1918, she accepted a position with the Massachusetts Mutual Life Insurance Company.[14] After fifteen years as supervisor of the women's department at MassMutual in Boston, she moved to England with her life partner, Ethel Bret Harte, daughter of the well-known novelist and poet Bret Harte. A year later, they drove across the United States and, in 1934, settled in Ojai, California, where both would spend the rest of their lives. Louise Hall died in 1966 at the age of eighty-five. Ethel Bret Harte had passed away two years earlier.[15]

By spring of 1915, the campaign was in full swing. On April 8 and 9, more than two hundred suffrage leaders representing all sixty-seven Pennsylvania counties met in Harrisburg for a conference to finalize their plans. A few days before the gathering, the *Allentown Democrat* reported:

> Every county in the state will be represented at this conference, and it is expected that the assemblage of women leaders from all parts of the commonwealth will be an eye-opener to those who have failed to note the development of the compact organization, which the women have been quietly building up during the past five years. For, despite the publicity, which

has been given to the suffrage movement, during that period, comparatively few of the voting citizens of Pennsylvania realize that in the women's suffrage party, the suffragists have perfected a statewide organization built upon the most approved party lines, with branches in 67 counties, and with legislative, borough, and ward leaders in every district where there are votes to be won. One session of the conference will be devoted to a full discussion of campaign propaganda. New literature, publicity, the tour of the Woman's Liberty Bell, and the extension of the "suffrage garden" idea are some of the concrete subjects that will be taken up.[16]

Katharine Wentworth Ruschenberger (1853–1943)

Katharine Wentworth Ruschenberger, ca. 1880.

Katharine Wentworth Ruschenberger, the visionary behind the Justice Bell, played a pivotal role in Pennsylvania's women's suffrage movement during the late nineteenth and early twentieth centuries. Born on November 2, 1853, in Philadelphia to John Langdon and Martha Emlen Wentworth, she grew up in Strafford, an affluent suburb of Chester County, as the eldest of four children. One of her sisters, Martha Wentworth Suffren, was also active in the suffrage movement in New York, working closely with Carrie Chapman Catt, a leading national suffragist who succeeded Susan B. Anthony as president of the National American Woman Suffrage Association.

In 1888, Katharine married naval officer Charles Wister Ruschenberger. They had no children, and she was widowed in 1908 at the age of fifty-five.[17]

Ruschenberger's lifelong dedication to women's equality is evident in her numerous leadership roles. In 1896, she was a member of the Women Suffrage Society of the County of Philadelphia, and by 1898, she was serving as the chair of the press committee for the Philadelphia Woman Suffrage Society. That same year, she represented the society as a delegate at the Pennsylvania

Woman Suffrage Association (PWSA) convention. She was also a member of the Equal Franchise Society of Philadelphia, an organization formed in 1909 by upper-class women advocating for suffrage.

Ruschenberger's contributions extended to the national stage in March 1913, when she coordinated with suffragist Alice Paul to feature a float carrying a plaster version of the Justice Bell in the Pennsylvania division of the suffrage parade in Washington, DC. In July of that year, she arranged for the same float and bell to appear in the Perry Centennial parade in Erie, Pennsylvania. A few months later, in November 1913, she arranged for the bell's appearance at a large suffrage parade in Brooklyn, New York, likely facilitated by her sister, Martha Wentworth Suffren.

Between 1913 and 1915, Ruschenberger tirelessly promoted the Justice Bell as a symbol of the suffrage movement. In 1915, she led the Chester County Woman Suffrage Party's publicity efforts, and that same year, at the age of sixty-two, she accompanied the Justice Bell during much of its statewide tour.

After the Nineteenth Amendment was added to the US Constitution, Ruschenberger remained dedicated to voting outreach and supporting women candidates, and was active in the League of Women Voters and the Republican Party. Katharine Ruschenberger died on February 11, 1943, at the age of eighty-nine.[18]

Victory!

On February 9, 1915, the Pennsylvania House of Representatives passed the suffrage amendment, and on March 15, the Senate followed suit. Amendment One would be on the ballot on November 2, 1915, and then it would be up to the voting men of Pennsylvania to grant or deny the women of their state the right to vote.

The suffragists had every reason to be hopeful that their campaign would pay off. Advance work had garnered substantial public support, and with seven and a half months until the election, they were ready to win the hearts and minds of the male voters.

What followed was a massive, well-coordinated campaign, as numerous suffrage organizations united under a single operation. The state was divided into nine districts, each to be led by a woman who would have several counties under her command. Four women were immediately secured as district leaders: Alice Kiernan (Mrs. E. E. Kiernan), Anna Orme (Mrs. Milton W. Orme), Kate Chapman (Mrs. Maxwell K. Chapman), and Mary Jackson Norcross. Because it was difficult to retain nine district leaders, additional organizers worked under the supervision of PWSA chair Hannah Patterson, and in many cases, especially in the smaller counties, a local suffragist would be in charge of her home county.[19]

With an estimated $100,000 needed for the statewide campaign, of which the Justice Bell tour was a part, the PWSA raised $78,698. This total included several large gifts, but the majority came from small donations. Women pledged money earned from selling fruit from their crops. One woman contributed $50 she had made by preparing numerous quarts of cottage cheese.[20] Counties held "Attic Days," during which people cleaned out their attics, sold the items at rummage sales, and donated the proceeds. Collections were taken up at street meetings and private events. Women offered overnight accommodations and meals for speakers, including the suffragists traveling with the Justice Bell.

The Speakers Bureau, managed by its secretary, Clarissa A. Moffitt, lined up some of the best orators in the country, including Alice Dunbar, a poet and journalist, and California labor activist Helen Todd. A publicity office led by Charles T. Heaslip employed three full-time writers and sent press releases and columns to 260 newspapers, while an army of suffragists fanned out across the state to help organize Votes for Women rallies and parades. An Allegheny County publicity department employed its own journalists and sent out weekly news bulletins to 500 newspapers, and from February to November, they also had a weekly cartoon service employing three cartoonists: C. D. Batchelor, Charles H. Winner, and Walter A. Sinclair. Wilmer Atkinson, president of the Pennsylvania Men's League for Woman Suffrage, supported the campaign, producing and distributing pro-suffrage literature throughout the state.[21]

In the meantime, the PWSA's crown jewel, the Justice Bell, was being prepared for its statewide tour, set to begin in June. Mounted on a specially modified car, the bell and a contingent of suffragists, led by tour director Louise Hall, planned to travel through all sixty-seven counties of Pennsylvania.

Casting a Symbol of Justice

Suffragists gather at Independence Hall in Philadelphia, March 30, 1915.

On March 30, 1915, Katharine Ruschenberger and other suffragists gathered in front of the Liberty Bell at Independence Hall in Philadelphia. From this symbolic location, they embarked on a train to Troy, New York, for the ceremonial casting of the Justice Bell. Press releases had been sent to promote the occasion, and reporters and photographers were on hand to record the event.

The *Evening Public Ledger* quoted Ruschenberger, who said, "We go from this sacred spot to cast a new national Liberty Bell, a woman's Justice Bell, which will ring to proclaim the completion of democracy through the enfranchisement of American women." Suffragist Lida Stokes Adams echoed this sentiment, saying, "Bells and banners are simply symbols of great and beautiful ideals and realities, but they helped to keep these ideals and realities ever present. The old Bell, [which] we all love, symbolizes freedom, without which there is no growth. The new Bell, which will be equally loved in the years to come, is to symbolize justice, without which there is no freedom, and no peace."[22]

Katharine Wentworth Ruschenberger at the Meneely Bell Foundrey, Troy, New York, 1915.

The suffragists did not miss an opportunity to make a spectacle, and the ceremonial casting of the Justice Bell was no exception. Twelve Philadelphia debutantes in white frocks were present, a PWSA banner was hung in the foundry, and Ruschenberger's niece, twelve-year-old Katharine Wentworth, the daughter of her brother, was on hand to pull the lever that released the molten bronze.[23]

The casting of the bell, speeches by suffragists from Pennsylvania, New York, and Massachusetts, and a banquet were all covered by the press. Scranton's *Tribune* reported on April 7 that the event even attracted movie companies:

> "Pennsylvania suffragists who were unable to make the trip to Troy, N.Y., to witness the casting of the Woman's Liberty Bell will soon have an opportunity to see the entire ceremony in the movies. Three of the biggest film concerns in the country had camera men at the Meneely Bell foundry when the casting took place, and they carefully recorded every step in the program from the time the Pennsylvania delegation left their hotel and were escorted by the Troy suffragists to the foundry, until the bell was cast and the white, hot mold was covered with sand by the workmen. Although 700 feet of film was used in taking the ceremonies, and the most picturesque features will soon appear on the regular 'news, weekly' reels sent out by the Pathé, Mutual, and Hearst-Selig film companies."[24]

Alas, those films have not been found.

Ruschenberger was interviewed by a reporter from the *Delaware County Daily Times*:

Katharine Wentworth Ruschenberger, 1915.

> For years, Mrs. Ruschenberger has been an ardent suffragist, working always with the firm conviction that the desire of women for the ballot was a just one and, for that reason alone, must prevail. How to visualize that conviction was another matter. But when the idea of the Woman's Liberty Bell came to her, she felt that the problem was as good as solved. This was a year ago. Yesterday the bell was cast in the foundry of the Meneely Bell Company at Troy, New York. . . . It will carry the words "Establish Justice." Mrs. Ruschenberger has ordered that clause added because in her opinion, "justice is the basic principle, upon which women as sharers in the burden of democracy finally rest their claim to enfranchisement."[25]

PART TWO

The 1915 Justice Bell Tour

Children with Justice Bell, New Wilmington, Pennsylvania, July 2, 1915.

Katharine Wentworth Ruschenberger with the Justice Bell,
Philipsburg, Pennsylvania, August 8, 1915.

The Road to Suffrage

It's hard to imagine now how unusual it was in 1915 to see women giving speeches, especially from a platform attached to a truck. As word spread about the Justice Bell, its clapper chained and silenced until women could vote, thousands of women and men traveled significant distances to see the famous bell and hear the suffragists speak. Among them was sixty-five-year-old Mrs. Sarah Grusel of Catawissa, Columbia County, who walked two miles in 97-degree heat. "You see," she told a reporter from the *Mercersburg Journal*, "I want the vote, and I want my daughter to have it, so I just naturally had to come along and let you know about it."[1]

Some women were so inspired by the Justice Bell that they ran for political office. In Lehigh County, Elizabeth DeGroot and Grace W. Kohler campaigned for school director positions in the 1915 election, becoming the first women in the county to do so. DeGroot won; Kohler lost by three votes.[2]

Suffragists found creative ways to encourage broad participation, including from children. While critics insisted women belonged solely in the home, organizers invited children to walk alongside them in parades—and parents brought them by the thousands. Many schools gave students the day off to see the bell. Some of the children who worked in coal mines, textile mills, and fields were granted permission to attend rallies.

In town after town, as the bell rolled into view, thousands of excited children waited, wearing their homemade sashes in suffrage colors—yellow or gold and white—ready to join the parades. They brought their musical instruments and played in bands, sang songs, and scattered yellow flowers over the bell. Boy Scouts often served as escorts and honor guards.

The two-thousand-pound bell proved an ideal attraction for children. Suffragists capitalized on their natural curiosity, inviting them to climb onto the truck and touch the bell. Many posed for photographs beside it. After the main speeches, the women would gather the children to hear stories about the old Liberty Bell and this new symbol of justice.

In Bellefonte, Centre County, forty children escorted the Justice Bell into town. In the small community of Duryea, Luzerne County, four hundred participated in the parade. In Lebanon, more than five hundred children joined the procession. And when the Luzerne County delegation handed the bell over to Columbia County suffragists, one thousand children joined hundreds of adults in welcoming it.

The 1915 campaign drew many women into state and national political activism for the first time, including Elizabeth McShane, who joined the Justice Bell tour when it passed through her hometown in Fayette County. Newspapers described her as one of the tour's most popular speakers. Later, she traveled to Washington, DC, where she was arrested and jailed for picketing in front of the White House in support of voting rights. McShane's journey from local activism to national protest was echoed by other women whose involvement in the campaign led them to continue their work on the national stage.

Although there is no record of Black women speaking from the Justice Bell truck's platform, they did participate in the 1915 campaign. The Pennsylvania Woman Suffrage Association hired Alice Dunbar (Mrs. Paul Laurence Dunbar), a prominent Black poet and journalist, as a speaker. Because Black men had gained the right to vote in 1870 through the Fifteenth Amendment, they could cast ballots in the November referendum. Dunbar traveled from her home in Wilmington to deliver speeches across Pennsylvania to both Black and White audiences, rallying support for the cause.

Alice Dunbar was just one of many Black women involved in the campaign. Others included Mary "Maize" Mossell Griffin of Philadelphia, chief officer of the suffrage department of the Northeastern Federation of Women's Clubs and president of the Sojourner Truth Suffrage League; Daisy Lampkin, president of Pittsburgh's Lucy Stone Woman Suffrage League; and Ethel "Etha" Carroll Cowles Armstrong, president of the PWSA's York County Negro Subcommittee. Armstrong was the driving force behind bringing Alice Dunbar to speak in York County, including for a well-attended event on the eve of the November 2 election.[3] Her sister, Clara Carroll Cowles, along with Georgiana Fulton and Susan Foster, were also notable members of the subcommittee.

While some Pennsylvania suffrage parades were integrated and some White women collaborated with Black women to varying degrees, most did not—a decision with lasting consequences that still reverberate today and that underscores the importance of documenting the full scope of the suffrage movement. The Further Reading section includes works that explore the vital role of Black women in the suffrage movement.

The Opposition

Those opposed to women's suffrage, known as the "antis" (pronounced *ant-eyes*), were prepared to do all they could to prevent Amendment One from passing on November 2, 1915. Among the larger forces the suffragists were up against were the well-funded liquor industry, which feared that women would vote for prohibition, and manufacturers, who worried that women would support child labor restrictions. Some men believed women were not intelligent enough to vote, while others feared that men would lose political power.

Some women also opposed women's suffrage. They viewed the political sphere as too corrupt for women, and they argued that women already held sufficient influence within their homes and families. Others believed that gaining the vote would make women masculine and undesirable to men.

Deborah Norris Coleman Brock (Mrs. Horace Brock), president of the Pennsylvania Association Opposed to Woman Suffrage, led the state's anti-suffrage movement. Under her leadership, the association exerted considerable influence across Pennsylvania through efforts that included sponsoring speeches, distributing literature, and lobbying legislators.

The antis found receptive audiences in counties populated by conservative Pennsylvania Germans, including Lehigh, Schuylkill, Lancaster, Berks, and York Counties. Despite this opposition, suffragists in these regions worked to build support, ensuring the Justice Bell tour was received by enthusiastic—or at least respectful—crowds. Newspaper accounts described some of the coldest receptions as happening in Lansdale and Montgomeryville, towns in Montgomery County. Schuylkill County, home to anthracite coal mines, textile manufacturers, and D. G. Yuengling & Son, America's oldest brewery, notably has no record of the Justice Bell's appearance.

As the Justice Bell made its way through Pennsylvania, the suffragists worked not only to confront entrenched views about a woman's role in society but also tailored their messaging to each county's specific concerns about voting rights. To help counter opposition arguments, the PWSA hired some of the most experienced speakers in the country, women who had already proven their ability to communicate eloquently and persuasively to diverse audiences.

Traveling through large cities, remote towns in the forested north, coal mining regions, and stretches of farmland, these speakers directly challenged anti-suffrage arguments in public forums. The PWSA sent Gertrude Breslau Fuller to Scranton to debate Claire Kulp Oliphant (Mrs. O. D. Oliphant) of New Jersey, a prominent anti-suffrage leader. Mary Stewart was called on to emphasize the benefits of enfranchisement in states where women could already vote, including her home state of Montana. Helen Todd, a nationally known labor activist, and Rose Winslow, a former child laborer, joined the PWSA's speakers' roster to address audiences in regions where boys were sent into coal mines and girls worked long hours in textile mills.

The liquor industry emerged as one of the most powerful opponents of women's suffrage, fearing that if women gained the vote, they would have the power to close saloons and pass a national prohibition amendment. Many women did, in fact, want to ban alcohol. Living in an era of limited rights, they were especially vulnerable to husbands and fathers whose alcoholism led to abuse or caused financial instability. Some women (and men) believed that alcohol encouraged immoral behavior and was, overall, a corrupting influence on society.

The Woman's Christian Temperance Union (WCTU), which had chapters throughout the country, was one of the most active organizations that promoted abstinence from alcohol. In Pennsylvania, Ella M. George, from Beaver County, was elected the state president of the WCTU in 1907 and held the position for twenty-two years. She supported women's suffrage, as did numerous other WCTU members, many of whom attended Justice Bell events.

While the suffragists had prepared for countering the opposition's arguments, there was one foe that caught them off guard: the weather. The summer of 1915 brought unusually heavy rainfall to Pennsylvania, with high temperatures and oppressive humidity adding to the discomfort. On August 3, torrential rain caused Erie's worst flood in one hundred years, and on August 21, a tornado tore through Hanover Township in York County, leaving destruction in its wake. The persistent rain turned dirt roads into mud, hampering the bell truck's progress and causing several breakdowns during the journey. These delays occasionally forced the women to cancel stops, much to the disappointment of those who had gathered to see the Justice Bell.

Still, the suffragists were indefatigable. The rain did little to stop their speeches or dampen their spirits, and they were rewarded by crowds in the thousands, with people arriving umbrella in hand, eager to see the bell and listen to the speakers. A typical account of audience persistence in the face of bad weather appeared on October 16, 1915, in the *Reading Times*, which reported on an event in Pennsburg, Montgomery County:

> Through rain and mud, the Woman's Liberty Bell came into the northern part of Montgomery County . . . . It rained while the addresses were being made in the Square at Pennsburg last night, and it came down in torrents in the afternoon. But the campaigners have made an inexorable rule not to postpone a meeting or cut out a stopping place on account of the weather, and they have kept faithfully to their schedule through the rain and heat and mud and the adverse weather conditions of the summer. So, when clouds broke and the rain came down, they simply hauled in their yellow flags, furled the red, white, and blue, let down the flaps of the auto truck, and went along the road like gypsies in a caravan.[4]

1915 Justice Bell Tour of Pennsylvania Maps

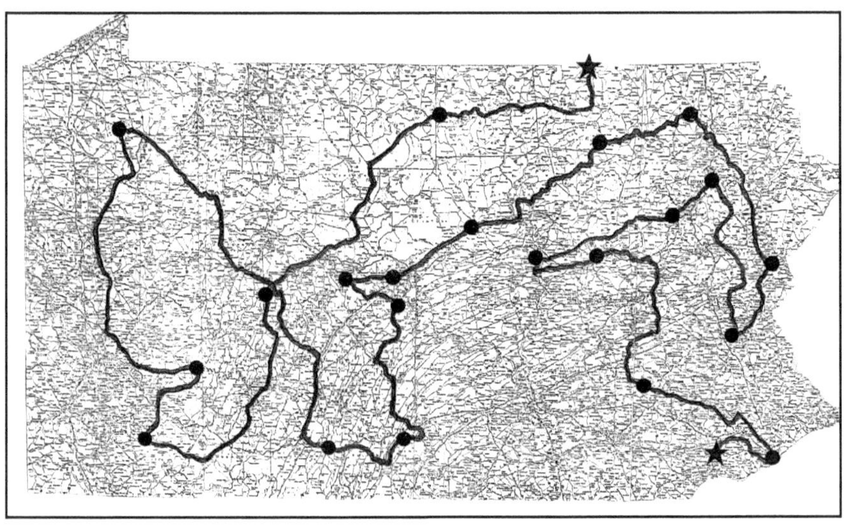

Map of the 1915 Justice Bell tour route,
constructed by Sara "Sallie" Corbishley, 1995.

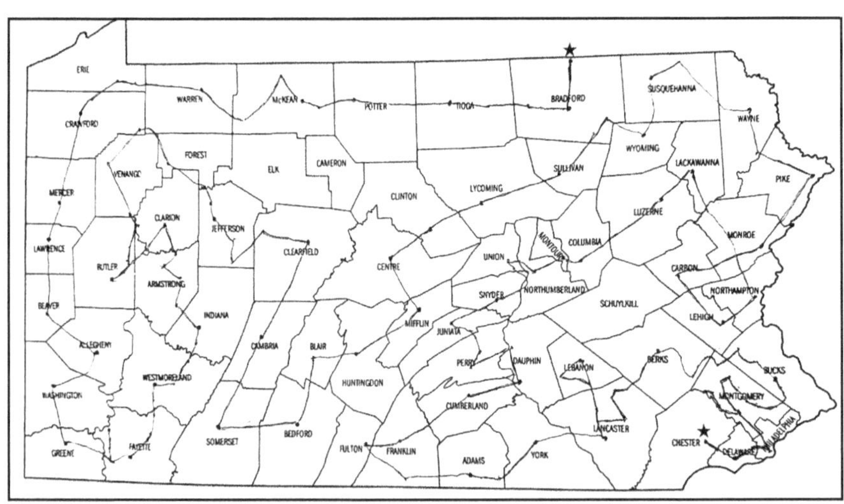

Map of the 1915 Justice Bell tour route,
reconstructed by Amanda Owen, 2025.

The Route

The route the women and the Justice Bell followed across Pennsylvania was meticulously planned, although a few adjustments were made as the start date approached, and sometimes the route was altered during the journey itself. A map drawn in 1995 by Sallie Corbishley, a League of Women Voters member, follows the locations as written on the sleeves of the glass-plate negatives found at the League's headquarters in Philadelphia. The dots on Corbishley's map represent those towns. The second map, with an adjusted and more detailed route, was reconstructed in 2025 by Amanda Owen, this book's author, and is based on newspaper accounts from 1915 that recorded the Justice Bell's travel.

The truck carrying the Justice Bell occasionally broke down, causing delays, and inclement weather further slowed the journey. As word of the bell spread, towns and cities not originally on the route requested visits, prompting the suffragists to adjust their schedule whenever possible to accommodate these eager audiences.

The Justice Bell tour did not extend to three counties. Although suffragists in Elk County appealed for a visit, there is no record of the bell entering either Elk or neighboring Cameron County.[5] Schuylkill County, known for its anti-suffrage sentiment, also appears to have been bypassed.[6]

As the route took shape, the suffragists followed a plan to travel from one county seat to the next, visiting smaller towns along the way. At each stop, they solicited donations and sold souvenirs, including small Justice Bells, watch fobs, calendars, and playing cards. At county lines, a convoy of automobiles formed a "guard of honor" for the Justice Bell, ceremonially passing it to suffragists from the next county.

The PWSA press department provided advance notice of the itinerary, giving towns several months to prepare parades and other events to welcome the bell. The seed packets that had been distributed earlier in the spring now bore yellow flowers—the suffrage color—an especially effective branding tool. As the suffragists arrived at their destinations, they were greeted by suffrage gardens in front yards, yellow bouquets in store windows, and fields shimmering with goldenrod.

The following pages trace the chronological route of the Justice Bell's journey across Pennsylvania. This section highlights key moments from each county, introduces the speakers, and presents newspaper articles documenting the bell's progress. These articles provide a record of the historic tour, capturing both its challenges and successes. While many towns welcomed the bell with enthusiasm and large crowds, some showed indifference or even resistance. Coverage also varied by county, with some newspapers publishing multiple articles while others offered only brief mentions.

The tour officially began on June 23, 1915, in Sayre, a small town in Bradford County along Pennsylvania's northeastern border. It concluded on October 30 in West Chester, the county seat of Chester County, where suffragists anxiously awaited the results of the November 2 election.

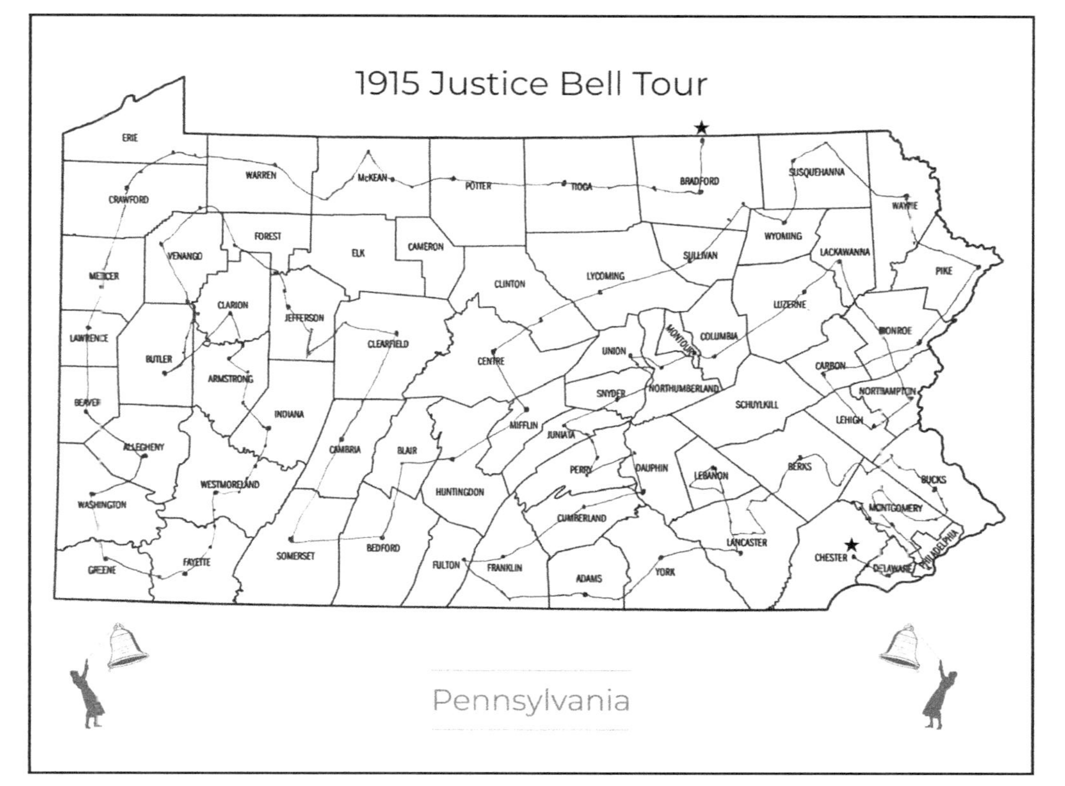

Map of the 1915 Justice Bell tour route, constructed by Amanda Owen, 2025.

JUNE 23–JUNE 30

Bradford, Tioga, Potter, McKean, Warren, Erie

Louise Hall and the Justice Bell near Gaines in Tioga County, 1915.

Highlights

On June 23, 1915, a large crowd gathered in Howard Elmer Park in Sayre, Pennsylvania, for the ceremonial sendoff of the Justice Bell's tour of the state. Katharine Ruschenberger formally presented the bell to the state's women, and Jennie Bradley Roessing accepted it on their behalf.

The journey would take the bell, and the suffragists accompanying it, through small towns and large cities, over mountains, and across miles of farmland. Residents across Pennsylvania were on alert, ready to welcome the two-thousand-pound bronze bell with its chained clapper.

This first leg of the tour through the sparsely populated northern counties was well organized. Suffragists had arranged rallies and locations to display the bell, as well as meals and accommodations for the travelers. At each county line, local delegations greeted the Justice Bell as it was handed over by representatives from the previous county. On June 24, the bell party arrived in Mansfield, Tioga County, where a crowd of one thousand attended an afternoon rally. The following day, musicians serenaded them in Gaines. Potter County suffragists, led by Eugenia Benn, chair of the county suffrage party, welcomed the bell on June 25 with parades of automobiles decorated with yellow streamers and banners. Louise Hall, the tour director, and Dr. Mary Wolfe, finance chairman of the Pennsylvania Woman Suffrage Association, were featured speakers.

The bell party spent three days in McKean County, from June 26 to 28, staying for two days in Bradford, home to suffragists Mrs. William Fry and Mrs. Guy Hill, who would travel with the bell party as aides through July. Eudora Ramsay, a suffragist from North Carolina, joined the bell party as a speaker in Kane. The Justice Bell arrived in Warren County on June 28, escorted into towns where the bells of courthouses and churches rang welcoming chimes for their silent sister bell.

Between towns, on the roadsides and at crossroads, people gathered to witness the unusual spectacle. The Pennsylvania Woman Suffrage Association's publicity efforts had ensured that citizens across the state were on the lookout for the enormous bell. The suffragists frequently stopped to deliver impromptu speeches to farmers and their families, and others who had come to see the traveling symbol of their cause.

By June 29, the bell party had reached Erie County. Despite torrential rain, five hundred people gathered in Union City to hear speeches by Dr.

Mary Wolfe, Louise Hall, Helen Todd, and local hero Augusta Fleming (Mrs. H. Neely Fleming), who had organized Pennsylvania's first suffrage parade in 1913. The first leg of the journey concluded on June 30.

BRADFORD COUNTY (June 23)

Woman's Liberty Bell Started on Statewide Tour: Suffragists Throng Sayre to See Their Trophy Begin Its Long Journey—Whole Town Turns Out

Sayre, Pa., June 23—Cheered on its way by a huge enthusiastic throng, the Woman's Liberty Bell was started from here this morning on its state-wide tour. A long string of gaily decorated automobiles filled with officers of the state suffrage association and leaders from all the neighboring counties, trailed after the big motor truck bearing the bell, giving the people of this county a picturesque demonstration of the enthusiasm, which is to mark the suffrage campaign in Pennsylvania from now on.

Although the ceremonies accompanying the start of the bell tour occupied less than an hour, they attracted one of the biggest crowds ever assembled here. In addition to the scores of suffragists who arrived from all parts of the state, every man, woman, and child in town who could get away from home, office or shop duties, hustled over to Howard Elmer Park, to see the official presentation of the bell to the state suffragists by its donor, Mrs. Katharine Wentworth Ruschenberger of Strafford.

The presentation ceremonies were both simple and effective. Mrs. Ruschenberger made a brief speech, in which she stated that the mission of the Woman's Liberty Bell is to establish justice for the women of the state by helping them to secure the same political independence which the old Liberty Bell proclaimed for the men. In her speech of acceptance for the state suffragists, Mrs. Frank M. Roessing, president of the Pennsylvania Woman Suffrage Association, explained the symbolism of the chains on the bell clapper, which are not to be removed until the day that the women of Pennsylvania are granted the right to vote.

Dr. George S. Carling, mayor of Sayre, extended the good wishes of the town people to the suffragists, and expressed the hope that their bell would accomplish its mission so well that it might peal forth its message to the women of Pennsylvania on the night of November 2.

After patriotic selections by the band, the big motor truck on which the bell is firmly lashed, was then slowly pointed westward. There was a blare of trumpets, a storm of cheers from the crowd, and the state-wide tour had started.
Times-Tribune (Scranton, PA), June 23, 1915

SUFFRAGIST SPOTLIGHT

Helen Todd (1870–1953)

Helen Todd, 1912.

Helen MacGregor Todd was born on April 1, 1870, in Shell Rock, Minnesota. She was one of four children of Robert MacGregor Todd and Salene Elmore Todd.[7]

By the time Helen Todd joined the Justice Bell tour in June, she had already gained national recognition for her suffrage work and her advocacy on behalf of workers, particularly women and child laborers. Newspapers praised her eloquence as a speaker and credited her with helping to secure the votes needed to pass California's women's suffrage referendum in 1911. Known as the "golden-tongued vote-getter," she popularized the slogan "We want bread, but we want roses, too," inspired by a poem by James Oppenheim. The phrase became a rallying cry of the American labor movement.[8]

Like many suffragists, Todd was shaped by her settlement work, including her time with Jane Addams at Hull House in Chicago. Concerned about the working conditions of women and children, she concluded that voting rights would enable women to improve their circumstances. She played a key role in introducing and passing California's minimum wage law for women in 1912 and was instrumental in securing passage of the state's motherhood pension law, which provided payments to impoverished single mothers to help them care for their children at home.

Todd was one of the Justice Bell tour's most popular speakers. She traveled with the bell party through many of the counties, concluding her participation in October with a speech in Chester County. That same year, she also campaigned in Massachusetts, where a women's suffrage referendum appeared on that state's ballot.

Helen Todd died on August 15, 1953, in New York City, at the age of eighty-three. A brief obituary in the *New York Daily News* noted that in addition to her contributions to the women's suffrage movement, she worked with Margaret Sanger to educate women about birth control and later helped secure city support for low-cost housing in Greenwich Village for creative artists.[9]

TIOGA COUNTY (June 24–25)

Suffrage Bell Travels Over Historic Highways

Wellsboro, Pa., June 25—The suffrage bell of justice has traveled in its two days' travel in northern Pennsylvania the old state road ordained by the legislature and built in 1807 from Towanda to Troy, thence into Tioga County, via Sullivan township and Mansfield, Covington and Blossburg to the county seat here. Tomorrow, the route of the old road will be resumed via Ansonia and Gaines to Galeton and Coudersport.

The Mansfield meeting today was a hummer. More than 1,000 persons cheered the equal suffrage speakers at the afternoon meeting. The ovation from the other towns was as hearty.

The bell arrived in Wellsboro and was met at the borough limits by suffragists and automobiles and escorted in, headed by a band. The town was gay with flags and bunting in honor of the event. The evening meeting was attended by hundreds of interested persons and the speakers were repeatedly cheered. Shrewd political judges say that it is safe to put Tioga County down in the suffrage column for a 1,000 majority.

Reading (PA) Times, June 26, 1915

POTTER COUNTY (June 25–26)

Suffrage Band Meets Woman's Liberty Bell

Coudersport, Pa., June 26—An Equal Suffrage Band, composed of 20 young musicians of both sexes, met the woman's liberty bell party at Gaines [Tioga County] yesterday, and serenaded it with patriotic selections. P. N. Dewey, the leader, proudly announced to the bell party that his four daughters and two sons were in the band and that they all hoped "to have a vote next year after the suffrage amendment has passed." The bell party was tipped off to the serenade awaiting it in Gaines by two women who hailed it from a field a few miles north of the town. The women looked at the bell longingly and said they wished they could go along to hear the speaking, but that the farm work could not be neglected. "You see," one explained, "our sons are playing in the band that's going to meet you at Gaines, and we are working at home in their places. We wanted them to play for you today, so that Tioga County could give you a big sendoff."

This incident made a deep impression on the bell party. Speaking of it later, Mrs. Frank M. Roessing, president of the State suffragists, said:

"No one can truthfully say now that the farm women of this State do not want the vote, nor that suffrage will make them either neglect their homes or their work. The sentiment displayed by the two women who sent their sons out to play in the band for us at Gaines is typical of that of all the Tioga County women who have helped to make our tour through that county so successful. We thank them most heartily and are more than glad that up here in the northern counties, suffrage sentiment is so strong."

Big ovations were tendered the bell party at all the towns through which it passed yesterday, including Gaines [Tioga County], Galeton and Coudersport [Potter County], where there was an automobile parade and a big mass meeting.

Seven automobiles filled with suffragists escorted the bell to Coudersport. Addresses were made by Dr. Wolfe, of Lewisburg, and Miss Louise Hall. Mrs. Eugenia Benn, county chairman, had charge of the party while in Potter County.

Evening Public Ledger (Philadelphia, PA), June 26, 1915

Mary Moore Wolfe (1874–1962)

Undated photograph of Mary Moore Wolfe.

Mary Moore Wolfe was born on March 31, 1874, in Lewisburg, Pennsylvania, one of four children of Charles Spyker Wolfe and Martha Elizabeth Meixell Wolfe.[10]

Mary Wolfe attained an exceptional level of education and professional standing for a woman of her time. She earned a B.A. and an M.A. from Bucknell University before graduating from the College of Medicine at the University of Michigan. Dr. Wolfe went on to have a distinguished career, serving as head of the Women's Division at Norristown State Hospital, a psychiatric facility in Pennsylvania, and as a professor at the Woman's Medical College of Pennsylvania.

In 1912, Wolfe became chair of the Pennsylvania Woman Suffrage Association's finance committee. Two years later, she and other suffragists founded the Woman Suffrage Party of Union County, with Wolfe serving as its first president. She joined the Justice Bell tour as a speaker in Tioga County and remained with the bell party through the end of June, delivering a speech in Erie County before departing. She rejoined the tour in late August and stayed through October.

Wolfe was appointed the first superintendent of the Laurelton State Village for Feeble-Minded Women of Childbearing Age, which opened in Union County in 1919. She served as its first superintendent until her retirement in 1940. Although she advocated for protecting patients from mistreatment, her leadership was rooted in eugenics, which aimed to prevent women deemed "defective" by the state from having children. Laurelton State Village officially closed in 1998.[11]

In her later years, Wolfe remained active in civic affairs, serving on local boards, including the Union County chapter of the American Red Cross during World War II. She died on October 18, 1962, at the age of eighty-eight.

MCKEAN COUNTY (June 26–28)

Suffrage Liberty Bell Visits Kane in Appeal for Votes: Welcome from Whole County

The bell has had a triumphal tour throughout McKean County. It was met Saturday morning at the McKean–Potter line by Mrs. T. M. Morrison, of Smethport, county chairman, and a party of suffragists. The bell was first escorted to Port Allegany. Most of the town's population heard the address. Crowds and interested attention have been evidenced in every town in the county where meetings were held. From Port Allegany, the bell was escorted to Smethport. Over 1,000 persons attended the meeting on the court house steps. Bradford suffragists met the bell at Smethport and at Colgrove. The biggest meeting of the day was held in Bradford on Saturday night in the public square. Addresses were made by Miss Hall and by Dr. Wolf.

Support Everywhere

Members of the party say that a spirit of cooperation is evidenced everywhere that they have been. It is shown in the eager faces of the crowds at every town and crossroad, in the cheers that have sped the bell on its way, in the pledges of men to vote "yes" for suffrage in November and in contributions for the "cause."

Such incidents make the suffragists confident of a victory on election day. A growing friendliness toward the proposal to give the ballot to women is found in every town. Favorable sentiment is found in large and small crowds alike. Everywhere they find a growing support which inspires optimism. The success of the tour gives confidence that the bell on November 2nd will ring out to "establish justice."

Kane (PA) Republican, June 28, 1915

WARREN COUNTY (June 28–29)

Warren Greets Suffrage Bell

Warren, Pa., June 28—Accompanied by automobiles, all tooting lustily on horns and sirens, the Woman's Liberty Bell, which is touring the state, arrived in Warren this evening. The bell was met at the county line by automobiles filled with exponents of the "Votes for Women" movement, among them

Mrs. James P. Rogers, president of the Y.W.C.A.; Miss Eva Jane Smith, and others.

After making stops in Sheffield and Clarendon, they arrived in the town of Warren for an evening rally with speakers Dr. Wolfe, Louise Hall and Eudora Ramsay. The bell group included Katharine Ruschenberger who had been following the bell in a touring car accompanied by Mrs. Davenport, chair of the Luzerne County committee, and Charles Heaslip, the publicity agent for the PWSA.

Pittsburgh Post-Gazette, June 29, 1915

Eudora Ramsay Richardson (1891–1973)

Eudora Ramsay Richardson, 1911.

Eudora Ramsay was born on August 13, 1891, in Versailles, Kentucky, one of three children of David Marshall Ramsay and Mary Woolfolk Ramsay. Eudora married Fitzhugh Briggs Richardson, an attorney, on December 13, 1917. Their only child, a daughter, was born in 1920.

Ramsay graduated from Virginia's Hollins University in 1910 and the University of Richmond in 1911, specializing in English language and literature. In 1912, she moved to Greenville, South Carolina, to take a job as the head of the English department at Greenville Woman's College, where she was known as a vocal supporter of women's suffrage. In 1913, she attended the national women's suffrage parade in Washington, DC, and in 1914, she was a founding member of a suffrage league in Greenville, the same year she received a master's degree from Columbia University.

In 1915, when Ramsay was the publicity chair for the South Carolina Equal Suffrage League, she briefly left her position to join the Justice Bell tour as one of its speakers, starting on June 28 in McKean County. She remained with the tour until July 22, when she gave a speech in Venango County.

For the next several years, Ramsay continued to work as a field organizer for the National American Woman Suffrage Association (NAWSA) in numerous states, traveling thousands of miles to help organize chapters and establish new local leagues. Later, she became an influential editor and author, writing several books and contributing to various journals and newspapers.

After the Nineteenth Amendment was added to the US Constitution in 1920, she continued to advocate for women. She served on the organizing committee of the Virginia League of Women Voters, helping to register women to vote, and traveled the country giving talks for women's organizations, including for the American Association of University Women and the National Federation of Business and Professional Women's Clubs. In 1937, she became state supervisor of the Virginia Writers' Project, part of the New Deal's Work Projects Administration.[12]

Eudora Ramsay Richardson devoted the rest of her life to her writing, becoming a well-known author and continuing to give talks on women's rights. She died on October 7, 1973, at the age of eighty-two.

ERIE COUNTY (June 29–30)

Suffragists on Tour with "Liberty Bell": Orators Address Mass-Meetings in Four Cities During Day's Run

Union City, Pa., June 30—Five hundred persons stood in the rain at a meeting in the city yesterday—a crowd said to have been the largest that ever assembled here at an outdoor meeting.

Among those who spoke were Dr. Mary Wolfe, state chairman of the Pennsylvania Suffrage Finance Committee; Miss Louise Hall, director of the bell tour; and Mrs. H. Neely Fleming, county chairman of Erie and vice president of the state suffrage association.

Mrs. Fleming was heartily applauded when she said "the State that has Independence Hall, the original Liberty Bell, and that was the first in the abolition movement should be the first of the 13 original states to enfranchise its women. I believe that the men of Pennsylvania in honor to themselves will give their women folk the ballot next November."

Evening Public Ledger (Philadelphia, PA), June 30, 1915

SUFFRAGIST SPOTLIGHT

Augusta Brown Fleming (1876–1949)

Undated photograph of Augusta Brown Fleming.

Augusta Agnes Brown Fleming was born on May 5, 1876, in San Francisco, California, to John William Brown and Agnes Ann Glasgow Brown. She married Hugh Neely Fleming in 1896 in New York, and by 1900, the couple had settled in Erie, Pennsylvania. Their only child was born there the following year.[13]

Fleming served as president of the Northwestern Pennsylvania Equal Franchise Association in 1913 and as a vice president of the Pennsylvania Woman Suffrage Association (PWSA) from 1913 to 1915. She was the driving force behind Pennsylvania's first suffrage parade, held on July 8, 1913, when suffragists from across the state gathered in Erie to form the women's suffrage division of the Perry Centennial parade. The parade marked the first appearance in Pennsylvania of the plaster Justice Bell, which was displayed on a float surrounded by suffragists in patriotic costumes.[14]

Ahead of the parade, Fleming wrote a letter to the women who would march. It was published in the July 6, 1913, edition of the *Erie Daily Times*: "To the Women of Erie: Gain a victory over fear and walk firm and erect on July 8 . . . . Remember that you are only one in a great army—that you are marching for a principle—and that government of the people, for the people, and by the whole people. Your motive is unselfish. You are trying to gain citizenship that you may do your part to bring about better legislation for the protection of the home, children, and the weak . . . . All women should feel the duty to pass on to their daughters the rich heritage of political freedom."[15]

Between 1913 and 1915, Fleming helped create suffrage postcards that were sold to help raise funds for the cause.[16] When the Justice Bell tour arrived in Erie on June 30, 1915, she delivered a speech from the bell truck's platform in the pouring rain to an appreciative crowd.

Following the ratification of the Nineteenth Amendment, Fleming remained active in civic affairs. She served for many years as president of the

Erie County Council of Republican Women and later completed two terms on the Pennsylvania Board of Labor and Industry.[17]

Augusta Fleming died on July 24, 1949, at the age of seventy-two.

JUNE 30–JULY 11

Crawford, Mercer, Lawrence, Beaver, Allegheny, Washington, Greene

Unidentified speaker with the Justice Bell, Sayre, Pennsylvania, June 23, 1915.

Louise Hall with the Justice Bell, Sligo, Pennsylvania, 1915.

Highlights

Rain trailed the bell party as it slowly made its way through Pennsylvania's western counties, navigating dirt roads turned to mud. When the group finally reached Meadville, the first stop in Crawford County, local suffragists warmly welcomed the weary, soaked travelers. That afternoon, the party continued to Cambridge Springs, home to a thriving suffrage society, where Mary Stewart, Dean of Women at the University of Montana, joined as a speaker.

Rain continued to plague the tour for much of the following week. In Mercer County, the combination of the one-ton bell and deteriorating road conditions caused the truck to break down, although the delay lasted less than a day. The bell party reached Lawrence County on July 2, where Pamphilia Hardman Phillips (Mrs. Thomas W. Phillips), president of the Lawrence County Women's Suffrage Party, was among those who welcomed the Justice Bell to the county. Local suffragists, in automobiles decorated in suffrage colors and adorned with "Votes for Women" and "Victory 1915" banners, accompanied the bell to New Castle, where a crowd of one thousand had gathered to hear speakers Louise Hall and Mary Stewart. Local newspapers hailed the event as the largest political rally in the city's history.

The bell party had until July 5 to reach Pittsburgh for the citywide National Americanization Day event in Schenley Park. Denied a permit to participate officially, the PWSA had spent weeks secretly planning a dramatic silent protest. With numerous stops still ahead, the bad weather and a truck breakdown forced them to skip some of the scheduled towns to avoid delaying their arrival.

Torrential rain fell as the Justice Bell arrived late in Beaver County on July 3, but the weather did not deter crowds from attending an outdoor rally to hear speeches by Mary Stewart and Louise Hall. No one wanted to miss their chance to see the bell. The following day, the party entered Allegheny County.

Lucy Kennedy Miller, president of the Equal Franchise Federation of Allegheny County, led the day's events when the bell party arrived in Sewickley on July 3. Festivities began with a procession of thirty decorated automobiles from Pittsburgh, Sewickley, and surrounding communities.

On July 4, the suffragists placed the bell at a designated location on Forbes Street between Schenley Park and the Schenley Theater. They set up a rest tent for women and children, while speakers addressed the public from the bell truck's platform and others organized the literature for distribution.

On July 5, as the National Americanization Day events commenced, the suffragists entered Schenley Park—and it was quite a spectacle. Hundreds of women, dressed in white with yellow sashes, marched silently into the park holding banners and came to a halt. They stood motionless as the crowd fell into an expectant hush, watching and waiting to see what would happen. Fifteen minutes later, without uttering a word, the suffragists departed just as they had arrived. The protest dominated newspaper headlines that day, just as the organizers had intended, drawing public attention to the women's suffrage movement.

Over the next five days, the bell party traveled through the final two western counties—Washington and Greene—drawing thousands eager to see the bell and hear the speakers, now joined by renowned Illinois suffragist Harriet Grim. On July 7, Margaret Brownson Linton (Mrs. Edwin Linton), chair of the Washington County suffrage party, received the Justice Bell in Monongahela on behalf of the county's suffragists. Two days later, the bell entered Greene County. After a rally in Waynesburg on July 9, the bell party spent the night there before departing the next day for Fayette County. They had now traveled through thirteen counties and hoped their efforts to shine a light on their cause would lead to victory on November 2.

CRAWFORD COUNTY (June 30)

Suffrage Bell Rides Through Mud on Tour: Orators Traveling with "Liberty" Emblem Enthusiastic Over Their Reception

Meadville, Pa., July 1—Defying muddy roads during a seven-hour trip from Union City, the Woman's Liberty Bell party arrived here last night and received a cordial welcome. Because of the conditions of the roads, the afternoon meeting at Cambridge Springs was announced as canceled, but when the party arrived a meeting of several hundred was quickly organized. Miss Louise Hall spoke, and John D. Gage, 82 years old, a prominent citizen, gave an address and read an original poem dedicated to the movement.

Mayor John E. Reynolds presided at the meeting here and addresses were made by Miss Mary Stewart and Miss Louise Hall, of the party. About 1,000 saw the bell and heard the speakers. Miss Stewart referred to the enthusiasm that has greeted the party on its first week out. Along the country roads, many farm houses bear suffrage decorations and small parties

have been out to greet the tourists.
Evening Public Ledger (Philadelphia, PA), July 1, 1915

SUFFRAGIST SPOTLIGHT

Mary Stewart (1876–1943)

Undated photograph of Mary Stewart

Mary Stewart was born on December 10, 1876, in Washington Township, Ohio, to Frank Stewart and Laura Forrest Stewart. By 1900, the family had moved to Loveland, Colorado. Stewart earned her A.B. from the University of Colorado in 1900, and over the next several years, she served as the principal of Longmont High School and later as a teacher at East Denver High School.

In 1907, Stewart moved to Missoula to become the Dean of Women at the University of Montana, where she taught languages. While there, she became active in the state's women's suffrage movement, which secured the vote for women in Montana in 1914.[18]

In 1915, Stewart wrote to the Pennsylvania Woman Suffrage Association to offer her help. "I feel that the women of Montana owe something to the women of the east," she wrote, "because without their help, we could scarcely have won our campaign last fall. It is in the spirit of gratitude, as well as devotion, that I am willing to give my services . . . for such a brief vacation as I have."[19] She joined the bell party as a speaker on June 30 in Crawford County and remained with the tour until August 7 in Centre County.

Stewart later moved to New York and attended New York University. In 1921, she relocated to Washington, DC, to take a position with the US Department of Labor. In 1935, she was appointed Assistant Director of Indian Education in the US Department of the Interior.

In addition to her suffrage work and other activities, Stewart was widely known for her poem and prayer "The Collect," written in 1904 while she was a member of the Longmont Fortnightly Club. The club was part of the General Federation of Women's Clubs (GFWC), which became the first national organization to adopt "The Collect" as a poem and prayer to be recited at official gatherings. The Federation of Business and Professional Women's Clubs later adopted it, and it has since been widely used by other organizations in the United States and other countries.[20]

Mary Stewart died on March 31, 1943, in Cincinnati, Ohio, at the age of sixty-six.

MERCER COUNTY (July 1)

> ***Suffrage Bell Has Covered 400 Miles***
>
> *Sharon, Pa., July 2*—The Women's Suffrage Liberty Bell has now covered more than 400 miles and has been cheered by more than 75,000 people in its trip through western Pennsylvania. The party leaves today for New Castle.
>
> The first accident of the tour occurred in Greenville yesterday, when one of the tension rods of the truck broke, necessitating repairs at the garage. The Mercer meeting was cancelled.
>
> The bell was the principal attraction in the Chautauqua parade here last night. The members were driven in automobiles over the principal streets, headed by a band. The open air meeting was attended by 1,000 people, a large part of whom were women. The addresses were delivered by Miss Mary Stewart of Montana, and Miss Louise Hall of Harrisburg. Their speeches were received with enthusiasm. Mrs. J. A. McLaughry, one of the candidates for the judgeship nomination in Mercer County, was in charge of the meeting.
>
> Mercer County members of the woman's suffrage party gave the party enthusiastic receptions at Greenville and Sharon. Traveling through a rich farming community, the bell attracted many farmers and their wives to the public roads to see it.
>
> The members of the party are enthusiastic over the trip and feel confident that it will result in much good.
>
> *Evening Public Ledger* (Philadelphia, PA), July 2, 1915

LAWRENCE COUNTY (July 2)

> ***Liberty Bell Greeted by Throng Here: Feminist Speakers Address Big Open Air Meeting on Diamond***
>
> With its wheels covered with several inches of mud, the big

truck bearing the Woman's Liberty Bell arrived in New Castle yesterday afternoon about 4 o'clock with a triumphal escort of local suffragists in automobiles who had met the party touring the state at New Wilmington and proceeded with them to the city, and last night the biggest political rally of its kind in the history of New Castle was held in the open air on the Diamond.

This morning local suffragists are jubilant over the demonstration that was accorded the [Woman's] Liberty Bell and its parties. The meeting and the attendant features were regarded as an augury of an awakened and quickened public spirit so far as the newer political movement is concerned.

Today the Bell is speeding on its way to Pittsburgh through Beaver County, where this afternoon meetings will be held, arriving in Pittsburgh for the supreme rally of the trip during July 4th. Everywhere the Bell has been greeted with acclaim according to the members of the party, and the northern tier of counties which were traversed on the way here are alive with a suffrage spirit.

New Castle (PA) Herald, July 3, 1915

BEAVER COUNTY (July 3)

Liberty Bell Comes in Drenching Shower: Reaches Beaver Falls One Hour Late and Program Is Changed to Suit

The Suffrage Liberty Bell was one hour late in reaching Beaver Falls Saturday. It arrived during a heavy downpour of rain. The Bell was displayed at the corner of Seventh Avenue and Fourteenth Street and was viewed by many people. Miss Louise Hall, the first speaker, gave a history of the original Liberty Bell, with special reference to the Suffrage Bell, and introduced Mary Stewart, of Montana.

The bell bears the inscription "Establish Justice, Proclaim Liberty, Secure the Blessing of Liberty Throughout All the Land to All the Inhabitants Thereof."

Accompanying the bell were ten ladies; among them Mrs. Ruschenberger, the donor, Mrs. Frank Roessing, state superintendent, and Miss Hannah Patterson, of Pittsburgh.

The ladies of the party were entertained at dinner at the Hotel Phillis by suffrage locals, members of which intended to hold an ice cream and strawberry festival at the close of the exercises, but

owing to the rain they sent the good things to the little folks at the Beaver County Children's Home in New Brighton.
Daily Times (Beaver, PA), July 6, 1915

SUFFRAGIST SPOTLIGHT

Hannah Patterson (1879–1937)

Hannah Patterson, ca. 1917..

Hannah Jane Patterson was born on November 5, 1879, in Smithton, Pennsylvania, one of seven children of John Gilfillan Patterson, a prominent banker, and Harriet McCune Patterson. She earned her A.B. at Wilson College in Chambersburg in 1901 and later studied law at the University of Pennsylvania, although illness prevented her from completing the program.[21]

Patterson settled in Pittsburgh, where she went on to become one of Pennsylvania's most influential suffrage leaders. In 1904, she co-founded the Allegheny County Equal Rights Association—later renamed the Equal Franchise Federation of Western Pennsylvania—and served as its second vice president. In 1912, she was elected auditor to the board of the Pennsylvania Woman Suffrage Association (PWSA) and helped develop the comprehensive political strategy known as the Pittsburgh Plan. In March 1915, she was part of a delegation of women who traveled to Troy, New York, for the casting of the Justice Bell. She later accompanied the bell party for much of its journey, serving as a support person and occasionally giving speeches.

In December 1915, Patterson was elected corresponding secretary of the National American Woman Suffrage Association (NAWSA). While continuing her suffrage work, she moved to Washington, DC, in 1917 to contribute to the war effort, accepting a position as director of the Woman's Committee of the Council of National Defense. She was later awarded the Distinguished Service Medal for her service during World War I.

By the late 1920s, Patterson had returned to Pittsburgh, where she remained active in civic affairs, including efforts to establish Allegheny

County's juvenile court. In 1931, she served as campaign manager for Sara M. Soffel, who became the first woman judge in Pennsylvania.

Patterson died on August 21, 1937, at the age of fifty-seven. The following year, Jennie Bradley Roessing commissioned artist Wayman Adams to paint a portrait of Patterson, which was presented to Wilson College in 1938. At the unveiling, Judge Soffel honored her, stating, "Those of us who knew her well, see her as the pioneer who walked in the sunlight and pointed the way; as the feminist who believed in women and sought for them equality of opportunity with men; as a leader in behalf of causes not yet won."[22]

ALLEGHENY COUNTY (July 3–6)

Women's Liberty Bell Is Welcomed to County

With clapper chained and padlocked, the Woman's Liberty Bell, replica of the historic emblem of freedom in Philadelphia, crossed the line into Allegheny County late yesterday afternoon.

Another lap of a long automobile journey through the state, to win sympathy and support for the cause of woman suffrage was begun. While Pittsburgh celebrates the 139th anniversary of the ringing of the first Liberty Bell, this silent symbol, upon the motor truck that bears it, will stand at Forbes Street and Grant Boulevard, a feature of the celebration.

Rain was falling when the bell crossed the line. As it came into view upon the road, it was greeted by the horns of a score of automobiles bearing suffragists of Pittsburgh and Sewickley. A brass band in a decorated auto truck swung into line ahead of it. One by one, the decorated cars of the welcoming suffragists took their place behind it. To the roll of drums and blare of brass, the procession entered Sewickley.

After parading the principal streets of the borough, the line of automobiles came to a halt in Broad Street, just below Beaver Avenue. The suffragists escorting the bell took their places about the truck. Mrs. John O. Miller [Lucy Kennedy Miller], president of the Equal Franchise Federation of Allegheny County, and Mrs. Frank M. Roessing [Jennie Bradley Roessing], president of the Pennsylvania Woman Suffrage Association, mounted beside it. Several thousand persons gathered to examine the emblem.

Mrs. Miller Speaks

"This bell," Mrs. Miller said in her preliminary address, "which will not sound until the men of Pennsylvania have given the women the right of franchise, could have come to us at no more appropriate time than on the eve of Independence Day. It must not be confused with the old bell in Philadelphia. That bell rang out liberty for men. This will ring equality for women. It is carrying a silent message all through the state, an appeal for the men to unloose its tongue, to let it proclaim that equality after the election in November. I am proud to welcome it to Allegheny County."

The principal speech at the Sewickley meeting was made by Miss Mary Stewart, dean of women at the University of Montana. She said in part:

"Fellow citizens and women of Allegheny County—I can address you men as fellow citizens, for in my state they recognize me as a citizen. It is my duty to speak for this bell that cannot speak for itself. Someday it will ring when you have given the women of Pennsylvania what the women of my state already have, the right to vote. You may all help to ring this bell, and when it rings you will have helped to make history. For its message will be heard farther even than the message that rang out your independence 139 years ago.

When women are given the vote, corrupt politics will no longer rule. Men's votes may be swayed at times, but women will think and vote for themselves. They will be as devoted to the good of the nation, as we are devoted to winning the right of franchise for them. Ours is not an easy task. We are campaigning an entire state. We are addressing thousands of persons and winning many of them who were until now opposed."

The bell party consists of Mrs. Frank M. Roessing, three speakers: Miss Louise Hall, Miss Mary Stewart, and Miss Harriet Grim; Miss Hannah Patterson, Mrs. Guy Hill and Mrs. William Fry, aids, and Charles T. Heaslip and Oliver Hall.

Pittsburgh Press, July 4, 1915

SUFFRAGIST SPOTLIGHT

Lucy Kennedy Miller (1880–1962)

Undated photograph of Lucy Kennedy Miller.

Lucy Kennedy was born in Braddock, Pennsylvania, on October 11, 1880, the eldest child of Julian Kennedy and Jennie E. Brenneman Kennedy. Her sister, Eliza, born nine years later, also became an advocate for women's suffrage. The family moved to Pittsburgh in 1890, where Lucy returned as an adult after graduating from Vassar College in 1902. She married John Oliver Miller on May 1, 1907, and was thereafter almost always referred to as Mrs. John O. Miller in newspapers and documents, as was the custom of the day. The couple had two daughters and one son.[23]

The women of Pittsburgh were among the most influential in Pennsylvania's campaign for women's voting rights, and Lucy Kennedy Miller stood at the forefront of the movement. In 1904, she joined Jennie Bradley Roessing, Hannah Patterson, Mary Flinn, and Mary Bakewell to form the Allegheny County Equal Rights Association (ACERA), which was renamed the Equal Franchise Federation of Western Pennsylvania in 1910.

During the Pennsylvania Woman Suffrage Association (PWSA) state convention in 1912, Miller was elected secretary of the association. In January 1914, she and Mary Bakewell established the School for Suffrage Workers, where University of Pittsburgh faculty taught more than one hundred women in courses on government and constitutional law, the legal status of women, taxation, and public speaking.

In July 1915, as the Justice Bell traveled through Allegheny County, Miller, then president of the Equal Franchise Federation of Allegheny County, led the activities for the bell and delivered speeches from the bell truck.

On November 30, 1915, Miller was elected first vice president of the PWSA board. Mary Thompson Orlady (Mrs. George B. Orlady) of Huntingdon was elected president, but illness prevented her from fulfilling her duties, leaving Miller to lead the organization, president in all but name. In November 1917, she was officially elected president.

Miller excelled in the world of politics. She was a formidable force and a gifted lobbyist for the PWSA, earning the respect of Pennsylvania politicians for her ability to stand her ground with the male legislators. She had boundless energy, impressive organizing skills, and a strong work ethic—all qualities that helped her raise money and expand the association's membership.

On June 24, 1920, when Pennsylvania legislators met to vote on the ratification of the Nineteenth Amendment, she became the first woman permitted by the men to address the legislature.

On November 10, 1920, the PWSA officially became the League of Women Citizens of Pennsylvania, later renamed the League of Women Voters of Pennsylvania. Miller remained state president, serving in that role until 1928.

In 1924, Miller once again traveled across Pennsylvania to register voters and educate women about their new political power. For the remainder of her life, she worked—often alongside her sister, Elizabeth Kennedy Brown—to combat corruption in Allegheny County and its county seat, Pittsburgh.[24]

Lucy Kennedy Miller died on June 30, 1962, at the age of eighty-one.

ALLEGHENY COUNTY (CONTINUED)

Silent Army of Suffrage Women March: Break In on Americanization Day Exercises Without Speaking: Carry Many Banners

Breaking in upon the Americanization Day observance in Schenley Park yesterday afternoon, with silent protest, representatives of the Equal Franchise Federation of Pennsylvania appeared in one of the most remarkable demonstrations ever seen in Pittsburgh.

In a long line they marched up around Flagstaff Hill—society women, business women, native-born women, foreign-born women, maids, matrons and grandmothers—all dressed in white with the yellow sash of the "Votes for Women" movement over their shoulders, and all silent in protest against the withholding from women the ballot. As score after score of the wordless protestants filed by, the throng of thousands assembled for exercises was hushed into silence as impressive as that of the marchers.

For 15 minutes they stood in a semi-circle about the edge of the crowd, holding aloft huge banners which spoke for them the sentiments they refrained from sounding. Then as silently as they had come, they wheeled around the hillside and marched away past Carnegie Institute, over the bridge into Grant Boulevard and down Forbes Street, where they had erected a big rest pavilion for women and children. Beneath the canopy was the suffrage Liberty Bell, brought in yesterday from Crafton where it had been exhibited following its arrival from a tour of half the state.

Attract Attention

The demonstration was a surprise to everyone except the participants, its unexpectedness and its perfect execution making it particularly impressive. During the time the women stood on Flagstaff Hill the attention of the crowd was theirs. Everyone waited to see what they intended doing and when they finally lifted their banners and silently moved away, the quiet of the throng was broken with the blended murmur of 5,000 voices in an exclamation of surprise.

The demonstration was planned, leaders said, after city officials had declined to issue them a permit for a pavilion in the park during the Americanization Day exercises.

Pittsburgh Post, July 6, 1915

WASHINGTON COUNTY (July 7–9)

Liberty Bell Arrived on Time: This Bell Will Ring for the First Time on the Day That Women of Pennsylvania Are Granted the Right to Vote

Amid the din of auto horns, gaily decorated cars and local suffragists wearing the conventional yellow, the color of the cause, the suffrage liberty bell arrived in Monongahela at noon today on time. The bell arrived at the east end of the river bridge where it was met by 25 autos, and was escorted across the bridge into Washington County. The parade continued down Main Street . . . to Chess and Fourth Streets where a large crowd had assembled.

Mrs. Edwin Linton, of Washington, PA, county chairman of the suffrage movement, received the bell for her cohorts in the county. Mrs. Henry C. Sutman, county vice president, introduced Miss Harriet Grim, of Chicago, a speaker of national fame, who for about thirty minutes discoursed on the advantages that would occur should the women be given the right of suffrage. She backed up her assertions by convincing facts and figures, and held her audience by her amusing anecdotes and stories which were interwoven into her subject that proved most convincing. At the conclusion she was met by a round of applause.

Miss Louise Hall, of Harrisburg, was called upon, but owing to the fact that she was suffering with a heavy cold and somewhat incapacitated, she confined her remarks to a short suffrage story which met the approbation of her audience.

After Miss Hall's remarks the meeting adjourned and the party was escorted to the Commercial hotel where dinner was served. At 2:30 o'clock the bell proceeded on its journey up the valley going to Donora, six autos from that place meeting the party in this city and acting as escort. A short meeting will be held there and at Monessen, and will then proceed to Charleroi where a large mass meeting will be held this evening.
Daily Herald (Monongahela, PA), July 7, 1915

GREENE COUNTY (July 10–11)

Suffrage Liberty Bell Is Busy: Sponsors Are Overjoyed at the Receptions It Has Been Given

Washington, July 11.—After a triumphant tour of two days and a half through Washington County, the suffrage liberty bell was taken into Greene County Saturday, arriving at Waynesburg early Saturday morning [July 10].

The suffragists are overjoyed with the receptions that have been accorded them through this section, and are confident that when the constitutional amendment, which grants the right of franchise to women, is voted upon in November, they will have shown a wonderful increase in their strength.

A demonstration was held in Waynesburg Saturday morning, an open air rally being held in front of the Court House. The throng of listeners was as big as that in Washington last evening, which was the record crowd since the tour was started.

Preceding the open air rally, an automobile parade was held in which prominent citizens of Waynesburg participated. A dinner reception in honor of the four workers accompanying the bell, Misses Hall and Grim and Mrs. Guy Hill and William Fry, was given by the members of the woman suffrage party of Waynesburg, with workers from all sections of the county in attendance.

The bell and party remained in Waynesburg all night, and were taken in the morning through the eastern section of Greene County and thence to Fayette, arriving in Uniontown early Sunday.

Reading (PA) Times, July 12, 1915

JULY 11–JULY 26

Fayette, Westmoreland, Indiana, Armstrong, Clarion, Butler, Clarion (second visit), Venango, Crawford, Warren, Forest, Clarion (third visit), Jefferson

Harriet Grim and the Justice Bell in Titusville, Pennsylvania, July 23, 1915.

Highlights

Over the next two weeks, between July 11 and 26, the bell party traveled through eleven counties. The first stops were in Fayette County, where a delegation headed by Frances White Umbel (Mrs. Robert E. Umbel), president of the county's suffrage party, arrived in Masontown to welcome the Justice Bell after it crossed the Monongahela River on a ferry. Among them was Elizabeth McShane, who later joined the tour as it passed through her hometown of Uniontown. In Perryopolis, the group was entertained at the home of Alfred M. Fuller, on a historic property once owned by George Washington. Fuller donated funds for electric lights to illuminate the bell and its platform for nighttime events.

By this time, the Justice Bell was so well-known that audiences of one to two thousand were common, even in areas where muddy roads made travel difficult. In anticipation of its arrival, local suffragists and town leaders planned parades, bands rehearsed, Boy Scout troops practiced cheers, and elaborate luncheons were prepared. Sleeping accommodations were arranged for the weary travelers, officials wrote speeches, and scores of automobiles greeted the bell party as it arrived to the sound of ringing courthouse bells.

As the bell party traveled from town to town, the suffragists were heartened by the warm receptions they received, especially after enduring bad weather, constant fundraising, and the physical strain of navigating long stretches of dirt roads. Without the benefit of microphones, even delivering speeches posed a challenge; the women had to project so forcefully that they sometimes lost their voices. Guest speakers from outside Pennsylvania provided much-needed relief for the regular orators, offering not only assistance with speeches but also helping to engage eager townspeople at every stop. Among them was Harriet Grim, superintendent of schools in Darlington, Wisconsin, and an experienced suffrage organizer. She had joined the tour in Pittsburgh and remained a featured speaker into early August.

Katharine Ruschenberger, traveling in a car with her own driver, frequently joined the tour. She gave occasional speeches and was warmly received by crowds who honored her for creating this symbol of equality. On July 13, in Greensburg, Westmoreland County, she joined Mary Stewart and Louise Hall to address a crowd of more than fifteen hundred. That evening, Ruschenberger hosted a reception at the Rappe Hotel, where local suffragists gathered to thank her for donating the bell to the cause.

In Indiana County, local suffragists joined Jane E. Leonard, president of the county's suffrage organization, to greet the bell party in Blairsville and escort them to the town of Indiana with stops in Blacklick and Homer City.

By July 16, torrential rains and flooded roads disrupted the Justice Bell tour, forcing the cancellation of several scheduled stops in Armstrong County's southern towns, Ford City, Freeport, Apollo, and Vandergrift. The following day, the suffragists continued their journey, stopping in Goheenville for a rally. From there, they traveled to New Bethlehem in neighboring Clarion County, where an evening meeting was planned.

At each stop, the suffragists continued to distribute literature and sell souvenirs to help fund their journey. In Petrolia, Butler County, a large turnout from the Women's Christian Temperance Union (WCTU), an organization sympathetic to the cause, greeted the bell party. Anti-suffragists were also active, distributing their own pamphlets at many events.

The bell truck broke down only once during this leg of the tour, on July 20, during a return visit to Clarion County. While Louise Hall and her brother, Oliver, stayed with the bell to arrange for its repair, the rest of the speakers continued into Venango County. Emma MacAlarney, a skilled speaker from Harrisburg, joined them there and remained with the bell party until the end of the tour. The repaired bell truck rejoined the suffragists in Venango County on July 22.

On July 23, the Justice Bell passed through four counties—Crawford, Venango, Warren, and Forest—before reaching Jefferson County on the evening of July 24. In Brookville, the bell was displayed near the courthouse. After resting on Sunday, the bell party resumed its tour with visits to Reynoldsville and Punxsutawney, concluding this leg of the journey.

FAYETTE COUNTY (July 11–13)

Dawson Greets Suffrage Bell: Gala Day When Suffrage Party Reaches the Town: Tour of Fayette County Is Closed

Dawson was one of the stopping places of the women's liberty bell and its escorts yesterday and the day in Dawson was celebrated as a holiday. The town was decorated in the national colors and in the yellow of the suffragists. Stretching across the street, where the bell entered the town, was a large streamer proclaiming the welcome the town extended to the bell and its followers. Mrs. N. A. Rist is the leader of the Dawson suffragists. Mrs. Rist worked continually and untiringly to make this meeting in Dawson a success. Mrs. Rist motored to Connellsville and met the bell and its party.

After the speaking, which was very ably handled by Miss Hall, of Philadelphia, and Miss Stewart, of Montana, ten young women sang several suffrage songs from an automobile and Miss Helen Bell Rush also sang several appropriate songs.

One of the features of the day was the parade of between 25 and 30 automobiles gaily decorated. The automobiles paraded the principal streets of the town and the occupants sang suffrage songs.

After leaving Uniontown yesterday morning, the party stopped in Dunbar and Miss Hall and Miss Stewart gave short talks and the party then moved on to Connellsville, where Miss Stewart was in charge of the speaking. The bell and escorts were accompanied as far as Connellsville by Miss Bess McShane and Miss Lenora B. Craft, both of Uniontown.

After the meeting in Connellsville, the party departed to Dawson and after the meeting in that city, the speakers and some of the visiting ladies to the extent of 75 were escorted to the home of Mrs. N. A. Rist, where they sat down to a beautifully appointed luncheon on the lawn of Mrs. Rist's beautiful home.

After the luncheon, the party of suffragists accompanied by the following Dawson people left for Scottdale: Mrs. N. A. Rist, Mrs. Roy Rist, Grace Moore, Margaret Snyder, and Mrs. Pallier. The automobiles these people were in as well as the autos of the speakers, were met on the boundary line of Fayette and Westmoreland Counties by the ladies from Scottdale.

Morning Herald (Uniontown, PA), July 14, 1915

SUFFRAGIST SPOTLIGHT

Elizabeth McShane (1891–1976)

Elizabeth McShane, senior-year portrait in the *Vassarion*, 1913.

Elizabeth McShane was born on October 9, 1891, at her grandfather's farm in Fayette County to Anna Dixon Vail McShane and William Wallace McShane. She attended Uniontown High School and, in 1913, graduated from Vassar College.

McShane joined the Justice Bell party on July 11, 1915, when the tour passed through her hometown in Fayette County, and later wrote in her diary, "Louise [Hall] asked me to join the crew, speaking at meetings, cross-roads, etc., urging people to ratify the Suffrage Amendment . . . . We campaigned over much of Pennsylvania, mostly on dirt roads, which became slippery when wet. We spent much time changing tires & trying to get the truck out of ditches."[25]

She remained with the tour as one of its most popular speakers until the final two weeks of the campaign, when the PWSA sent her to Philadelphia to work with Mary Ingham, founder and board member of the Equal Franchise Society of Philadelphia. "In Philadelphia, we spoke on street corners, held meetings, called on voters, distributed literature, etc."[26]

After the campaign, McShane was offered a job working with Ingham at William P. Bonbright & Co., a securities firm in Philadelphia. In 1917, both women joined other suffragists in Washington, DC, to picket in front of the White House as part of a campaign, led by Alice Paul, to fight for a federal women's suffrage amendment. Many of the picketers, including McShane, were arrested and incarcerated on a fabricated charge of "obstructing traffic."

In her secret prison diary, which was smuggled out while she was still incarcerated, McShane wrote on November 16, 1917, "Now eight days on a hunger strike. Very weak and ill. Fainted yesterday afternoon in cell. Forcibly fed some hours later. Food poured into a vomiting stomach. Left in cell all night unattended. Fainted and was found at 5 o'clock on the stone floor."[27] The forced feedings continued, despite a physician's diagnosis of stomach ulcers. Before her release on November 27, McShane developed a gallbladder infection.[28] She was one of many suffragists who were abused by the prison guards during their incarceration.

McShane spent the next several years studying chemistry and biology at Bryn Mawr College, and she later worked in fields related to industrial diseases, including at Massachusetts General Hospital in Boston in 1921. Ingham, who had been living in Philadelphia with McShane, moved with her to Boston, where they purchased a home together.

In 1924, McShane married William Hilles. The couple had two daughters and divorced in 1938. McShane went on to teach high school in Massachusetts, Rhode Island, and Pennsylvania.

During her later years, she was active in many organizations, including the American Civil Liberties Union, the Friends Committee on National Legislation, and the League of Women Voters. Elizabeth McShane died on August 13, 1976, at the age of eighty-four.[29]

WESTMORELAND COUNTY (July 13–14)

Woman's Suffrage Bell Attracts Large Crowd Upon Its Visit Here

With banners flying and streamers streaming, the Woman's Suffrage Bell, escorted by a company of prominent Suffragists, came to Latrobe for a little visit this morning, and it was accorded a hearty reception by a big crowd.

A portion of the escorting delegation arrived a little ahead of the bell and, without wasting any time, Miss Louise Hall, of Harrisburg, addressed the crowd, telling something about the bell and the idea behind it. She also spoke about the Suffrage question, referring to several phrases of it. She declared, in answer to the argument that the right of suffrage would take women away from home, to the neglect thereof, that in all her travels she had not found a man who would admit that voting had ever necessitated any neglect of his business.

With the coming of the Bell, Attorney James B. Weaver, representing the borough government, welcomed it and the visiting delegation. He spoke briefly, but forcibly, concerning the inherent right of Woman to possess the ballot, and he asked that it be given to her as a matter of right, under the constitution, and in accord with all principles of justice.

Miss Harriet Grim, of Illinois, made a most pleasing impression upon the crowd. Witty and charming, presenting her statements of fact with sureness and boldness, and yet with true womanliness, she captured the hearts of the audience, as well as the minds, and opened up pocketbooks, too, quite a liberal response being made when the collection for the good of the Cause was taken up.

The Bell attracted a lot of attention while on view, and the forcibleness of its silenced clapper was not lost.

Accompanying the party to Latrobe was Mrs. Katharine Ruschenberger, of Philadelphia, the donor of the bell. She is paying, also, the expenses of the tour on which it is being taken.

From here the Bell was taken to Derry, a delegation of Derry ladies escorting it to the neighboring town.

Latrobe (PA) Bulletin, July 14, 1915

INDIANA COUNTY (July 14–15)

The Bell Was Here: Woman's Suffrage Liberty Bell and Escort Here Wednesday Evening and Given Enthusiastic Greeting

With the old Court House Bell ringing a welcome to its new and silent sister, the Woman Suffrage Liberty Bell, escorted by leading suffragists of the state, and automobiles filled with the adherents to the cause in Indiana, arrived in Indiana Wednesday evening at 5:40 o'clock. Quite a number of persons had gathered to see the emblem of women's rights, which remained in front of the Court House for a few minutes and then headed the procession down to the BR&P station and back to the center of town, where the parade disbanded and from where the party was taken to the homes of Mrs. R. A. Thompson and Mrs. Margaret Blair of Schumacher for dinner.

The forty minutes missed in the run from Blairsville to Indiana, made the mass meeting in front of the courthouse forty minutes late in starting, but the enthusiasm was there and the Court House square was crowded with persons who came to hear what the speakers had to say. Previous to the opening of the meeting, the Indiana Military Band played several selections, ending with

"America," as the bell rounded the Sixth Street corner.

The customary suffrage arguments were given in a clear and concise manner by Miss Harriet Grim, of Illinois; Miss Louise Hall, of Harrisburg; and Miss Mary Stewart, of Montana. Their remarks were right to the point and were listened to with the greatest of interest. One of the important witnesses to the meeting here was Mrs. Katharine Ruschenberger, of Strafford, near Philadelphia, the donor of the bell and who is paying all the expenses of the tour. Other members of the party were: Mrs. W. P. Frye and Mrs. Guy Hill, of Bradford and Mr. Oliver Hall, chauffeur, of Harrisburg.

During the course of the speeches, suffrage literature and souvenir pins of the bell were distributed. That the Antis were not napping during the Indiana meeting, was shown by the hundreds of anti-suffrage pamphlets that were distributed through the audience.

Thursday morning at 10 o'clock the Bell party left for West Lebanon, and from thence to Apollo, Vandergrift, Leechburg and Freeport, where at the latter town a mass meeting was held last evening.

Indiana (PA) Weekly Messenger, July 21, 1915

SUFFRAGIST SPOTLIGHT

Harriet Grim (ca. 1885–1967)

Harriet Elizabeth Grim, 1912.

Harriet Elizabeth Grim was born in Fulton, Illinois, on February 25, sometime between 1881 and 1885, to Ephraim W. Grim and Elizabeth A. Jones Grim.[30] She entered the University of Chicago in 1904. By her twenties, Grim was already nationally known for her suffrage work, and on May 27, 1908, she was a guest speaker at the National American Woman Suffrage Association's sixtieth anniversary convention in Seneca Falls, New York.[31] In June of that same year, she was selected to introduce the women's suffrage plank at the Republican National Convention—a selection that drew considerable attention. The *Ottumwa (IA) Tri-Weekly Courier* reported on June 16, 1908, "The honor of facing the political solons is unique for a girl scarcely out of her teens. At the university, Miss Grim won a considerable reputation, both as an orator and as an advocate of women's suffrage."[32] The proposed plank read: "We recommend the granting of suffrage to women upon the same terms which is granted to men." It was rejected. Grim went on to organize in multiple states, including Illinois and North and South Dakota. NAWSA placed her on salary as an organizer for the Wisconsin Woman Suffrage Association through which she helped establish several new suffrage groups to support the fight for a women's suffrage amendment in the state. (The referendum for Wisconsin state suffrage failed in 1912.)

Grim later served as a superintendent of schools in Darlington, Wisconsin, and continued her work as an organizer for both the Wisconsin Woman Suffrage Association and NAWSA. Offering to assist the Pennsylvania suffragists during her summer break, she joined the bell party in Pittsburgh on July 4 and remained with it until early August, delivering numerous speeches throughout the western counties.

In 1927, Grim earned a master's degree from the University of Wisconsin, followed by a doctorate in 1938. (Her dissertation was on Susan B. Anthony.) She became head of the speech department when Professor Gertrude Johnson retired in 1944, a position she held until her own retirement in 1952. Grim and Johnson are listed as partners in the same household in the 1940 and 1950 censuses. Harriet Grim died on September 7, 1967.[33]

ARMSTRONG COUNTY (July 16–17)

Liberty Bell Party Stops Called Off Due to Bad Roads

Kittanning, Pa., July 16—Many towns in the southern part of Armstrong County, where the Women's Suffrage Liberty Bell had been scheduled to stop today on its tour of the state, were doomed to disappointment as a result of the roads being practically impassable for the heavy truck carrying the bell. Heavy rain storms in that section Wednesday and Thursday flooded the roads, and the stops at Ford City, Freeport, Apollo and Vandergrift were called off, and the party came here directly from Rural Valley.

Stops were made today at Elderton and Rural Valley after

leaving Indiana. More than 2,000 persons attended the meeting here tonight. The bell will be taken to Goheenville, Armstrong County tomorrow morning where addresses are scheduled for noon. The party then will go to New Bethlehem [Clarion County] where a meeting will be held tomorrow evening. The party will stay over Sunday in New Bethlehem.
Pittsburgh Post-Gazette, July 17, 1915

CLARION COUNTY (July 17–18)

Suffragist Bell Greeted at Clarion: Party Will Stay There Until Tomorrow Morning When Tour Proceeds

Clarion, Pa., July 17—Local suffragists in automobiles, several hundred business men and other residents accorded the women's suffrage Liberty Bell and party a rousing reception upon their arrival here tonight.

The [Woman's] Liberty Bell party was two hours late arriving here owing to bad roads, caused by the heavy rains. The bell and party left Kittanning, Armstrong County, this morning, stopping at Goheenville and several small towns in Clarion County, and arriving at New Bethlehem at 3 o'clock this afternoon.

Mrs. W. S. Hipple, president of the New Bethlehem suffrage party, heading a large delegation, met the party on the outskirts of the town. Following a parade through the principal streets, a public meeting was held in Broad Street. Addresses were given by Miss Harriet E. Grim and Miss Louise Hall, members of the party, and local suffragists.

More than 1,000 persons, the majority voters, attended the meeting. The party left New Bethlehem at 4 o'clock, arriving here two hours later.

The visitors will remain in Clarion over Sunday and are scheduled to leave here early Monday morning, making their first stop at Sligo. They will proceed to Rimersburg, then to East Brady, where they will stop for luncheon. The party will arrive in Butler County Monday afternoon, making the first stop at Chicora.
Pittsburgh Post, July 18, 1915

BUTLER COUNTY (July 19–20)

Karns City Gives Bell Warm Welcome

Butler, Pa., July 20—A committee of 12 of the Butler County Suffrage Association, headed by Mrs. E. J. Hickson, chairman, escorted the Woman's Suffrage Liberty Bell on its trip through Butler County today. The party left Butler this morning and made its first stop in Chicora, where they were greeted by a small crowd, a heavy rain holding down attendance. The speakers were Katharine W. Ruschenberger, the donor of the bell, and Miss Harriet E. Grim.

The biggest reception of the day was given at Karns City where the suffrage bell party was met by school children carrying flags and a committee of Karns City suffragists.

At Petrolia, the party was met by the Woman's Christian Temperance Union, which turned out in a body to greet the bell. The town was decorated and a large crowd was present to hear addresses by Miss Louise Hall and Miss Grim. At Bruin, the last stop in Butler County, a large demonstration was held in honor of the bell.

Following the meeting at Petrolia, the Butler suffragists returned home. The next stop of the bell was in Foxburg where the party was well received. The party arrived in Emlenton this evening and will spend the night here. A large crowd attended tonight's meeting.

Pittsburgh Post, July 21, 1915

CLARION COUNTY (July 20–22)

Woman Suffrage Bell in Trouble

The Woman Suffrage Bell is having its troubles, but it is expected that Franklin people will get a look at it tonight or tomorrow. Shortly after the party left Foxburg this morning, the truck bearing the bell broke down and it was at the side of the road for several hours. It was finally taken to Turkey City, where it is being repaired under the direction of Miss Louise Hall, state organizer for the Woman Suffrage Party.

Owing to the mishap, the speakers did not reach Oil City until 2:30 this afternoon. They were: Mrs. Katharine Wentworth Ruschenberger, who furnished the bell and made the state tour possible; Miss Grim of Illinois; and Miss Eudora Ramsay, of Greenville, S. C. Miss Anna L. MacAlarney, of New York, joined the party in Oil City this afternoon.

At 3 o'clock a street meeting was in progress on Seneca street, Oil City, the speakers being Miss Grim and Miss MacAlarney. There is a large crowd.

After the speech making, the campaigners will go to the Business Girl's Club for lunch and then proceeded to Franklin, with a short stop at Reno. An evening meeting will be held at 12th and Liberty Street, with the Rocky Grove Band furnishing the music.

With the state speakers are a number of Franklin and Oil City women. Mrs. C. K. Brown, who is county chairman, accompanied several Oil City women to the Clarion County line and met the campaigners. Several others drove to Oil City this afternoon.

There is nothing certain when the repairs on the motor truck will be finished, but it is expected that they will be done in time to get to Franklin tonight or in the morning.

News-Herald (Franklin, PA), July 22, 1915

VENANGO COUNTY (July 22)

Large Crowd Hears Suffrage Speakers

Franklin Pa., July 23—The Woman's Suffrage Bell got an enthusiastic reception in Franklin last night. Several hundred men and women attended an open meeting near the bandstand, and listened to addresses by three of the women accompanying the bell. The large number of men present was probably the most striking feature of the meeting.

The bell, which was at Foxburg from Tuesday night until Thursday afternoon on account of an accident to the steering gear on the motor truck, arrived in Franklin about 5:30 o'clock, and was exhibited to hundreds of persons last night. The speechmaking was from a platform on the rear of the truck.

The Woman Suffrage Party is fortunate in having the services of such splendid speakers as those who addressed the crowd here last night. They are talented women and good orators, and the fact that they do not resort to abuse but logical argument augurs well for the cause.

Message of the Bell

Miss Eudora Ramsay of Greenville, South Carolina, the first speaker, brought the message of the Liberty Bell. She spoke of the old Bell and this message. "The present campaigners are bringing another bell without a crack like the old one, a bell which the voters can make to ring out on the night of November 2.

"The old bell rang out as a protest against taxation without representation. And the new bell is also a protest against that which the forefathers declared to be tyranny. Let it ring," said the speaker, "and let the whole past know that Pennsylvania has paid a great tribute to its womanhood.

"True democracy," the speaker said, "has been tried and proved successful . . . Taxation without representation is tyranny, and women are taxed. This is supposed to be a government of, by, and for the people, and women are people."

News-Herald (Franklin, PA), July 23, 1915

VENANGO, CRAWFORD, WARREN, FOREST, CLARION, JEFFERSON COUNTIES (July 23–24)

Suffrage Bell Back in Campaign

Franklin Pa., July 22—The woman suffrage bell got back into the campaign for votes for women today after being disabled for two days, the truck having broken down Tuesday night at Foxburg. Brief stops were made at the country villages of Salem, Clarion County, and Nickleville and Reno, Venango County, and well attended meetings, were held at Oil City and Franklin [Venango County]

The itinerary for the remainder of the week: Titusville [Crawford County], Tidioute [Warren County], Tionesta [Forest County]; Saturday, Newmansville, Tylersburg, Scotch Hill [Clarion County], Sigel and Brookville [Jefferson County]. Sunday will be spent in Brookville.

Pittsburgh Post-Gazette, July 23, 1915

Suffrage Bell Party in Forest County

Brookville, Pa., July 24—The Suffrage Liberty Bell party arrived here late this afternoon and was given an enthusiastic reception. The party left Tionesta, Forest County, this morning, making stops at Nebraska [Forest County], Tylersburg, Scotch Hill [Clarion County], and Sigel [Jefferson County], where addresses were made by the suffragists. Fully one thousand men and women were at the open air meeting tonight and heard addresses by Miss Harriet Grim of Chicago, Miss Emma MacAlarney and Miss Louise Hall, both of Harrisburg, PA.

The party will spend Sunday quietly in Brookville. Reynoldsville, Punxsutawney, and DuBois, and the smaller places will be visited on Monday.

Pittsburgh Daily Post, July 25, 1915

SUFFRAGIST SPOTLIGHT

Emma Lenore MacAlarney (1871–1925)

Emma Lenore MacAlarney, 1915.

Emma Lenore MacAlarney was born in Harrisburg in August 1871 (exact date unknown) to Elmira "Ella" Hoffman MacAlarney and Joseph MacAlarney, an attorney. Her uncle, Mathias MacAlarney, served as editor and publisher of the *Harrisburg Telegraph* newspaper.[34]

MacAlarney graduated from Wellesley College in 1892 and later taught at the Horace Mann School of Columbia University. She used her privilege to advocate for women's suffrage, founding several suffrage leagues in Pennsylvania towns and organizing local groups in numerous counties. A gifted speaker, she put her talent to use traveling with the Justice Bell, beginning in July in Venango County.

The *Daily Republican* newspaper reported on a speech she delivered to several hundred people in Phoenixville on October 14, 1915: "In spite of the threatening clouds, Miss Emma L. MacAlarney, of Harrisburg, did not disappoint the local suffragists last night. . . . [Her] unusually excellent delivery attracted an audience of several hundred people, and her clear convincing argument held them all interested until she finished. She is an exceptionally talented speaker, and is devoted heart and soul to the cause, so her sincerity as well as her brilliant mind makes her unusually persuasive."[35]

She remained with the bell party, delivering numerous speeches through the end of the tour in Chester County. Afterward, she returned to her home in New York, where she continued to support women's causes. She taught at several schools and also worked for the *New York Sun* as an editor and the writer for its "Woman Who Saw" column. Later, she served as principal of the Washington School in New York City.

Emma MacAlarney died on September 11, 1925, at the age of fifty-four.

JEFFERSON COUNTY (July 24–26)

> ***Woman's Liberty Bell in Brookville***
>
> The Woman's Liberty Bell and the party accompanying it, reached Brookville last Saturday afternoon, toward evening. The auto truck carrying the bell was halted in Pickering Street, near the court house, where it was viewed by hundreds of our citizens. The bell is a handsome one, an exact copy in every way of the old Liberty Bell that has hung so long in the State House in Philadelphia. It was mounted on a strong auto truck, but so arranged that it could not be rung. It is not to ring until the voters of the State give the right of suffrage to the women of the State, and then its joyous notes will ring out loud and clear.
>
> A great crowd, one of the largest audiences we have ever seen in Brookville, assembled around the band stand on Pickering Street at 7:30 in the evening to hear the ladies speak. Good order was preserved, and the meeting was well conducted and orderly in every way. Burgess Shields extended a hearty welcome to the ladies, and assured them a generous and sympathetic hearing. Three addresses were made. The speakers were introduced by Mrs. W. N. Conrad, who is at the head of the suffrage movement in Brookville. The addresses occupied in all about an hour. The speakers occupied the bandstand, and the large audience surrounded them on every side.
>
> Miss Grim, a schoolteacher of Chicago, was first speaker. Her address occupied about twenty or twenty-five minutes, and was a model in diction and manner of delivery. It was an elegant address, and carried conviction to many hearers. Her address would have been a credit to our congressional halls. She hails from Chicago, where women vote.

Miss MacAlarney, of Harrisburg, was the second speaker, occupying a little more than twenty minutes of time. Her address was nicely delivered, and well received.

The last speaker was Miss Hall, of Harrisburg. She is a very fine talker, but was tired and made her address short.

These ladies are among the best public speakers we have heard in many a day. They presented the suffrage question in its best form. Their arguments were good and all their illustrations apt. The meeting was an entire success, and it ought to be helpful to the suffrage cause in Jefferson County.

Jeffersonian Democrat (Brookville, PA), July 29, 1915

JULY 26–AUGUST 4

Clearfield, Cambria, Somerset, Bedford, Blair

Betty Bratton with the Justice Bell in Somerset, Pennsylvania, July 30, 1915.

The Justice Bell tour, Pennsylvania, 1915.

Highlights

The women had much to celebrate as they drove into DuBois in Clearfield County on July 26. A little more than one month after departing Sayre, the Justice Bell had completed its first one thousand miles.

Continuing south through farm country, the bell party passed houses decorated in national and suffrage colors, and when it stopped in towns and cities, the meetings drew enthusiastic audiences. The Justice Bell arrived in Ebensburg in Cambria County on the evening of July 28, and, as in so many towns, the suffragists were greeted by the ringing of the courthouse bell and a band playing patriotic music. Speeches by Harriet Grim and Louise Hall captivated the audience with impassioned arguments that outlined both the practical reasons why women should be able to vote and the broader issue of fairness.

Throughout the tour, speakers stayed for varying lengths of time, with Louise Hall and Elizabeth McShane remaining the longest. In Somerset County, Harriet Grim left the tour for previously scheduled engagements, and Susan FitzGerald (Mrs. Richard FitzGerald), a suffragist from Massachusetts, joined the bell party. She remained with the group until August 11.

Somerset County was home to Alice Kiernan (Mrs. E. E. Kiernan), an influential organizer appointed by the PWSA as district leader of six counties. She hosted the travelers overnight in her home and coordinated events throughout the county. On July 30, as the bell came into view just outside Somerset, she led a long procession of automobiles filled with suffragists to escort it into town, where she and Louise Hall delivered speeches to a crowd of one thousand.

When the bell truck broke down on July 31, delaying a visit to Meyersdale, Kiernan sprang into action and organized an evening rally without the bell. Louise Hall addressed an audience of five hundred.

The challenging weather that had plagued much of the tour persisted. By the time the now-repaired bell truck entered Bedford County on August 1, the rain had returned, and a heatwave that had gripped the state for days brought oppressive humidity and stifling temperatures in the 90s. A torrential downpour on August 2 made conditions even worse, leading officials to declare it the most devastating flood in the county's history—a calamity mirrored in other parts of Pennsylvania, with Erie experiencing its worst flood in one hundred years on August 3.

The bell party persevered and arrived in Bedford on the morning of August 3 to find a large crowd waiting for the travelers. Louise Hall stood on the bell truck's platform, umbrella in hand, and delivered her speech.

More mechanical trouble with the bell truck temporarily delayed progress after the suffragists entered Blair County on August 3, but they reached Altoona for a late-day rally and spent the night there. The following morning, a parade featuring the Justice Bell drew a crowd of one thousand. Susan FitzGerald joined Louise Hall and Mary Stewart to deliver the speeches.

On August 4, thousands of farmers and their families gathered for a picnic near Henrietta, a small town in the southeastern corner of Blair County, to hear Alice Kiernan and Claire Kulp Oliphant (Mrs. O. D. Oliphant), a national anti-suffrage speaker, present their views on women's suffrage. Oliphant criticized the Justice Bell. "I want to say that it is a counterfeit bell: a gigantic joke. Last night in Altoona, Louise Hall sneeringly said the original bell is a half-cracked bell, and that there is no crack in the woman's liberty bell. I resent that characterization of our precious liberty bell.... The suffrage speaker said, 'That cracked bell only gave liberty to the men of the State.' Such a statement as that is not only foolish, but treasonable."[36] Skilled suffrage speakers—and Kiernan was among the best—readily countered anti-suffrage sentiment, turning gatherings into opportunities to advance their message and win over new supporters.

During this leg of the tour, the bell party had faced breakdowns of the bell truck, widespread flooding, stifling humidity, and oppressive summer heat. Yet their spirits remained remarkably high, bolstered by camaraderie and the generosity of local supporters who did everything they could to ensure the success of each visit.

CLEARFIELD COUNTY (July 26–27)

> ***Women's Liberty Bell Complete First Thousand Miles of State Tour***
>
> *Dubois, Pa., July 27*—The Woman's Liberty Bell arrived here last evening, completing the first thousand miles of its tour of the State. Since its start from Sayre, in Bradford County, on June 23, the huge bronze symbol of the women's appeal for political independence has passed through 21 counties and visited 162 towns and cities. Approximately half a million people have seen it and assisted in the enthusiastic receptions that have greeted it all along the route.

Going through the farming districts, the bell party has found house after house daily decorated with both the national and the suffrage colors, and crowd after crowd gathered at each crossroads to see the bell and hear the corps of women speakers accompanying it explain its message.

In the industrial districts, many factories have taken half an hour recess in order to let the men see the bell and hear the suffrage speeches. The mass meetings held in all towns and cities where noon and night stops have been made, have been successful both from point of attendance and enthusiasm.

After leaving here, the bell will travel south through Cambria and Somerset Counties. It will then zigzag up and down the state, passing through practically every county between now and the election. When it completes its trip in Philadelphia on the Saturday before election, it will have traveled approximately 5000 miles.

Allentown (PA) Leader, July 27, 1915

CAMBRIA COUNTY (July 28–29)

Suffrage Liberty Bell Here Wednesday Night: Left at 10 O'clock Thursday Morning: Large Crowd Turned Out to Welcome Bell and Hear the Speakers of the Evening

The [Woman's] Liberty Bell arrived in this place Wednesday evening [July 28] about three hours after schedule time. The band was out early to welcome the party and helped to make the occasion a memorable one. Several hundred people gathered on our streets and patiently awaited the arrival of the bell. The advanced guard reached here about 8 o'clock, and the meeting was at once opened.

A. W. Buck introduced the first speaker Miss Harriet E. Grim from the state of Illinois. Miss Grim held the closest attention of the large crowd that assembled. She is a forcible speaker and drew much applause from her hearers. She argued for the cause and pleaded for votes in favor of equal suffrage at the coming election.

About 9 o'clock the long looked for Bell arrived. The crowd had not dispersed. A. W. Buck introduced the next speaker, Miss Hall from the state. She entered at once into a discussion of her theme and advanced arguments for the cause she represented. She also commanded the closest attention, and at

the conclusion of her address asked those who would support equal suffrage to raise their hats. She found many of her hearers in sympathy with the movement. The party left here at 10 o'clock Thursday morning, and spent the day in touring other towns in the county.
Mountaineer Herald (Ebensburg, PA), July 30, 1915

SOMERSET COUNTY (July 30–August 2)

Woman's Liberty Bell Was Delayed: But Rousing Suffrage Rally Was Held Just the Same Saturday Evening

The Woman's Liberty Bell failed to arrive in Meyersdale at noon last Saturday, as per schedule, its arrival being delayed until Monday afternoon [August 2] on account of a breakdown of the auto truck on which it is being transported throughout the State. The truck was laid up in Somerset over Sunday for repairs.

The bell's arrival at Somerset Friday evening [July 30] was hailed with great acclaim. Many automobiles decorated with the suffrage colors, white and yellow, escorted it into town. A meeting was held in front of the court house at which addresses were made by E. E. Kiernan, Esq., Miss Louise Hall, and Hon. J. A. Berkey. About 1000 people were present. Miss Harriet E. Grim of Wisconsin, who accompanied the bell on a speaking tour for four weeks, left it at Somerset and returned West to keep other engagements. The bell tourists were entertained at the Kiernan farm during their stay at Somerset.

Meyersdale suffragists were ready for the reception of the bell Saturday noon, but were disappointed on account of the breakdown at Somerset. On being urged to have a rally here on Saturday evening, in spite of the non-arrival of the bell, Mrs. E. E. Kiernan [Alice Kiernan], who is chairman of six counties of Pennsylvania, including Somerset, for the suffragist cause, and Miss Louise Hall, custodian of the bell, came over in the Kiernan car, driven by Edmund Kiernan, Jr., and a rousing meeting was held at the bandstand after supper.

The Citizens Band played for the ladies, and a crowd of about 500 people collected around the bandstand to hear the music and the speaking. After several selections by the band, the editor of the *Republican* made a few preliminary remarks and introduced the first speaker, Miss Louise Hall, director of the Woman's Liberty Bell tour. Miss Hall is a very attractive young woman and an effective stump speaker. She delivered an excellent address and soon had the crowd with her. Although she had much noise to compete with, made by passing automobiles and street cars, she nevertheless made herself heard above the din and evoked frequent salvos of applause. There can be no doubt that her speech helped the cause.

After Miss Hall had concluded, Mrs. Kiernan made a few remarks and offered for sale Liberty Bell watch fobs, scarf pins, etc. at 10, 15 and 25 cents, for the benefit of the cause. A collection was also taken up from the crowd and many of the men in the audience contributed liberally. Mrs. Kiernan and Miss Hall returned to Somerset after the meeting.

On Monday morning [August 2], the Liberty Bell started again on its journey from Somerset. The roads were soft and slippery in many places from recent rains and progress was slow. It was nearly 2 o'clock when the bell arrived at Meyersdale with Miss Louise Hall and her brother, as chauffeur, in charge, and two young ladies accompanying them.

The truck halted in front of the Slicer House while the members of the party repaired to Zinn's restaurant for dinner. A large crowd congregated around the bell truck, to view the beautiful emblem of liberty. The tongue of the bell is chained and will not be unloosened until the women secure the ballot, when it will proclaim the glad tidings throughout the state.

After refreshing themselves and selling some badges, the bell tourists proceeded on the way to Berlin. They had scarcely gotten out of town when a very heavy rain descended, and they had to stop to put chains on the tires and let down the curtains of their vehicle in order to avoid a severe drenching.

The bell arrived at Berlin about 4:30 o'clock where a large crowd was waiting to greet it. Many decorated automobiles met it at the outskirts of the town and escorted it to the lower diamond where Miss Hall delivered a rousing address, and stirred up enthusiasm to a high pitch. After the speaking, escorted by a number of decorated automobiles filled with suffragists, the Woman's Liberty Bell proceeded on its journey, headed for Schellsburg, Bedford County. Its passage through Somerset County was like a triumphal procession, thousands of

people having turned out to speed it on its journey and to listen to the able advocates of woman's suffrage who told the mission of the bell.
Meyersdale (PA) Republican, August 5, 1915

SUFFRAGIST SPOTLIGHT

Alice Kiernan (1870–1953)

Alice Kiernan, ca. 1900.

Alice Flack Kiernan was born in Pittsburgh, Pennsylvania, on June 15, 1870, to Julius Flack and Nancy Paisley Flack. She married Judge Edmund Earl Kiernan on March 27, 1895. They had two children and made their home in Somerset, Pennsylvania.[37]

On March 20, 1913, the first women's suffrage meeting in Meyersdale, Pennsylvania, took place with Alice Kiernan presiding. After that meeting, an equal suffrage club was formed and officers were elected. The group soon became a branch of the Pennsylvania Woman Suffrage Association (PWSA), ready to support the legislative effort to place a suffrage referendum on the ballot. That same year, Kiernan was elected as an alternate at the National Suffrage Convention in Washington, DC. By 1914, she was the PWSA's Division Eight district leader with six counties under her command: Huntingdon, Bedford, Somerset, Cambria, Fayette, and Blair.

In anticipation that the legislature would pass the suffrage amendment for a second time in early 1915, paving the way for a popular vote, Kiernan hosted a planning meeting at her home on July 10, 1914. Between two hundred and three hundred women gathered to hear speakers, including Jennie Bradley Roessing and Hannah Patterson, and to coordinate campaign efforts.[38]

By the time of the Justice Bell tour in 1915, Kiernan was recognized as an effective and influential suffrage leader in Pennsylvania. When the bell party passed through Somerset County between July 30 and August 2, she gave speeches and hosted the traveling suffragists at her home. The following summer, in July 1916, hundreds of suffragists again assembled for the dedication of a specially designed state suffrage flag. At the time, Kiernan was serving as vice president of the PWSA Executive Committee.[39]

After Edmund Kiernan's death in 1925, Alice Kiernan and her son moved to Laguna Beach, California, sometime in the 1930s. She lived there until her death on June 18, 1953, at the age of eighty-three.

BEDFORD COUNTY (August 2–3)

Woman's Liberty Bell: Reached Bedford Tuesday Morning: Address on Public Square

The Liberty Bell on its tour through Pennsylvania reached Bedford Tuesday morning [August 3], instead of Saturday evening as expected. The cause of the delay was a broken truck and the heavy storm that made the roads impassable for travel. On arriving here, the truck containing the bell went immediately to the Bedford Garage, where an enthusiastic crowd greeted it. Miss Louise Hall, a state speaker, with two other workers, and her brother, who acted as chauffeur, composed the party.

Standing on the truck with the Liberty Bell, Miss Hall, delivered a very excellent and enlightening speech on women's suffrage . . . . She answered all arguments against women suffrage in a very telling way. From here the bell went by the way of Osterburg and Fishertown to Altoona, where a great demonstration awaited it.

Bedford (PA) Gazette, August 6, 1915

BLAIR COUNTY (August 3–4)

Suffrage Bell Given Ovation Here

The Suffrage Liberty Bell, the members of the escorting party, and the distinguished speakers with the bell, received an ovation as they moved through the city last evening. The parade formed on Thirteenth Avenue and Twelfth Street and was more than four squares long, forty automobiles being the parade. Bright yellow, the suffrage color, was everywhere in evidence. Cars were decorated with suffrage pennants, banners, golden glow, sunflowers, and the occupants of the cars wore yellow flowers and ribbons.

Mrs. Susan FitzGerald of Boston, daughter of Admiral

Walker, was the first member of the visiting party to speak. She said: "I have come down to help my Pennsylvania sisters win for themselves the right that we women of Massachusetts so much covet for ourselves."

Her entire address was simple and direct, and was addressed particularly to the voters of the Keystone state. Mrs. FitzGerald made quite a hit with the men of the audience as she made her argument for the cause, which she so earnestly and eloquently advocated.

Louise Hall, the brilliant young suffragist, made a fine appeal for the cause of equal suffrage, telling many humorous incidents that kept the crowd in good humor, and at the same time illustrated startling facts that brought the necessity for women's suffrage home to the logical, thinking men of her audience.

Miss Mary Stewart, dean of the University at Missoula, Montana, made the closing address of the meeting, which was received with enthusiastic applause. She said:

"The industrial conditions of the world have changed. The home is no longer the industrial center and our interests have followed our work to the factory, the store, the place of business. We women did not desire to meddle in politics until politics first meddled with us.

"The question of equal suffrage is not a woman's question, but is a question of fundamental justice. The woman's movement is the outgrowth of democracy, the growth of civilization, which seeks to place on the individual the responsibility for civic welfare.

"I have never heard a man say that he was willing to represent a woman at the tax collector's office. He is only willing to represent her where her judgment, will, caprice and selfishness can be expressed. Is a man willing to let others think for him or vote for him? The reason a woman desires to vote is exactly the same reason that has made men through countless ages struggle and demand the right to express their opinion in forming the government under which they must live."

Miss Stewart and, indeed, all of the speakers were heartily applauded, and the rain did not succeed in dampening the enthusiasm of the crowd in the least.

The members of the escorting party will leave for Juniata this morning and from there to Tyrone.

Altoona (PA) Times, August 4, 1915

SUFFRAGIST SPOTLIGHT

Susan FitzGerald (1871–1943)

Susan FitzGerald, ca. 1910.

Susan Grimes Walker was born on May 9, 1871, in Cambridge, Massachusetts, to Rear Admiral John Grimes Walker and Rebecca White Pickering Walker. She graduated in 1893 from Pennsylvania's Bryn Mawr College with a degree in political science and history and later served as assistant to the college's president. On August 3, 1901, she married Richard Y. FitzGerald. The couple had four children and, by 1911, were living in Boston. Like many suffragists, FitzGerald worked in New York City settlement houses. From 1901 to 1904, she served as resident head of Richmond Hall Settlement. She later became a member of the New York Child Labor Committee.[40]

By 1915, FitzGerald was an experienced speaker who had traveled to numerous states to assist with suffrage campaigns, including in 1912 when she joined Louise Hall, a fellow Massachusetts native, to campaign for a women's suffrage referendum in Cincinnati, Ohio.

When she joined the Justice Bell tour as a speaker on August 3, 1915, in Blair County, FitzGerald was serving as executive secretary of the Massachusetts Woman Suffrage Association and as recording secretary of the National American Woman Suffrage Association (NAWSA), a position she had held since 1911. She remained with the tour until August 11, giving her final speech in Clinton County.

In 1920, FitzGerald served as an alternate delegate from Massachusetts at the Democratic National Convention in San Francisco. Two years later, she was elected to the Massachusetts House of Representatives as one of the first two women to serve in the state legislature. She died on January 20, 1943, at the age of seventy-two.[41]

AUGUST 4–AUGUST 12

Huntingdon, Mifflin, Centre, Clinton, Lycoming

Louise Hall speaking at the New York Central Shops in Avis, Pennsylvania, August 11, 1915.

An unidentified speaker addresses a crowd from the back of the truck carrying the Justice Bell, 1915.

Highlights

As the Justice Bell and suffragists traveled through central Pennsylvania from August 4 to August 12, newspapers reported no rain or mechanical problems with the bell truck. The improved weather was a boon for the tour, which now drew even larger crowds to rallies held on "the Diamond," a common term used for large outdoor areas that served as a town's focal point, such as a public square. Louise Hall continued to lead the bell party as director, with Elizabeth McShane, Susan FitzGerald, and Mary Stewart serving as the main speakers for this leg of the tour.

On August 4, the Justice Bell traveled into Huntingdon County. In the town of Huntingdon, the county seat, the evening program featured a children's performance and a Black drum corps playing patriotic marches. As in many towns, audience members gave liberally to support the tour. On August 6, in Matawanna, Mifflin County, Elizabeth McShane climbed a fence at the Cross Roads stores to give a speech and was rewarded with generous donations.

On August 7, forty young girls dressed in yellow and white helped pull the bell into Boalsburg, Centre County. Elizabeth Blanchard Beach (Mrs. Robert Mills Beach), chair of the county suffrage party and a vice president of the PWSA, joined Hannah Patterson, Susan FitzGerald, and Mary Stewart in accompanying the bell to State College. Later that evening, a crowd of 2,000 gathered in Bellefonte to see the bell and hear speeches by FitzGerald and Stewart.

The Justice Bell spent three days in Clinton County, concluding with a stop at the New York Central Shops in Avis, where Louise Hall addressed a large crowd of workers. In Williamsport, the turnout was one of the largest in Lycoming County's history. The attention surrounding the bell and the suffragists included an interview with Oliver Hall conducted by Helen Hoyt, a woman reporter—a rarity at the time.

HUNTINGDON COUNTY (August 4–6)

Liberty Bell Draws Well: Suffs Hold Stirring Meeting Around Symbol of Political Freedom

Great crowds greeted the Suffrage Liberty Bell and its band of speakers at various points in the county yesterday and today. Yesterday's tour of the county ended in an open air meeting held here around the big truck carrying the huge bronze bell. The Diamond was well filled.

The bell was late in its arrival here, and long before it appeared, people thronged Penn Street for a couple of blocks. Among the noticeable features of the evening was a colored drum corps, playing patriotic marches with great gusto. Its music seemed to typify the fight the women of Pennsylvania are making for liberty, and if one stretched his imagination, it was remindful of the famous picture of the three tattered heroes of the Revolutionary war, "The Spirit of '76."

Huntingdon has many citizens, friends of the suffrage movement. That was shown by the manner in which nearly everyone responded to the request that flags be hung out in honor of the visit of the Liberty Bell.

When the auto truck, bearing the bell which the women hope to ring for freedom in November, arrived at the outskirts of town, a number of automobiles, trimmed in suffrage yellow, formed a convoy for it.

The speakers uttered their appeals from the front of the auto truck that bore the symbol of their hope. One woman had traveled from Montana to participate in the Pennsylvania campaign. She was Miss Mary Stewart, dean of the University of Missoula, Montana. She had her subject well in hand, and proved a shrewd, clear-minded thinker, a clever entertainer, and her earnestness lent a decided force to her address. She was applauded again and again. We'll wager there isn't a man in the whole state of Montana that casts his ballot with a greater degree of intelligence than Miss Stewart.

The other speakers were Rev. C. W. Sheriff, pastor of the Baptist church, and Mrs. Susan FitzGerald of Boston, daughter of Admiral Walker. Mayor George W. Fisher welcomed the suffragists to Huntingdon, and introduced the first speaker of the evening.

With flags floating [and] with the Suffrage Liberty Bell held silent in expectancy of victory in November, looming up behind the speakers, the very air seemed surcharged with a spirit of freedom—freedom for the fairest creatures of the Keystone State—its women. After hearing the speakers, after granting to be true the arguments they advanced, one was instilled with a great deal more genuine patriotism than usual when a bevy of little boys and girls lifted their voices in song, the main sentiment of which is "Sweet Land of Liberty."

A collection was lifted in the large crowd to be turned over to the Liberty Bell crusade. The collection was liberal.

Huntingdon (PA) Globe, August 5, 1915

MIFFLIN COUNTY (August 6)

Big Demonstration for Suffrage Bell: Woman's Liberty Bell Stops at Lewistown Today on Tour of the State

Lewistown, Pa., August 6—The Woman's Liberty Bell touring Pennsylvania in the Votes for Women campaign, arrived in this place today and was accorded a great welcome. Miss Martha Cummings, Mrs. J. Harlan Landes, Mrs. Frank Mann, and Mrs. Bessie Long, officers for Mifflin County of the PWSA motored to Ellen Chapel to meet the bell, which is traveling on a powerful motor truck accompanied by a group of women workers in the cause. The bell was escorted over the principal streets of the town by a number of automobiles loaded with well-known citizens.

This evening at 7:30 o'clock speeches will be made on Monument Square by visiting suffrage speakers, where thousands of pieces of literature will be distributed to the assemblage. The Reverend G. M. Walker, pastor of the Baptist Church, a speaker of ability, will give a brief talk.

Miss Mary Stewart of Montana, and Mrs. Richard FitzGerald of Massachusetts, will speak from the court house steps. Miss Stewart is dean of the women's department of the University of Montana, [and] Mrs. FitzGerald is the daughter of Rear Admiral Walker, and one of the most prominent social betterment workers of her sex. Before her marriage, she was head of Fiske Hall, Barnard College.

Harrisburg (PA) Telegraph, August 6, 1915

CENTRE COUNTY (August 7–8)

40 Children Parade with Suffrage Bell

Bellefonte, Pa., August 7—Not in its trip so far through the state did the woman's suffrage Liberty Bell get such an ovation, as was given it in Boalsburg, Centre County, this afternoon when 40 little girls gaily bedecked in white and yellow hauled the bell into the town. Two dozen young women acted as a guard of honor.

To Theodore Davis Boal belongs the credit of this generous reception. The bell and its suffrage contingent were met exactly at the county line on the seven mountains by County Chairman Elizabeth Blanchard Beach, Miss Mary Gray Meek, Reverend G. E. Hawes and others. The first stop was in Potters Mills, where a good size crowd of farmers heard Mrs. FitzGerald warmly espouse the cause of suffrage. At Center Hall, luncheon was served the party of 40 or more by Miss Florence Rhone, daughter of Leonard Rhone.

Then came the big reception at Boalsburg. State College also turned out a big crowd, but the banner meeting was in Bellefonte this evening when 2000 people viewed the bell and listened to the talks of Mrs. FitzGerald and Miss Mary Stewart. The entire party is enthusiastic over Centre County's reception, and especially the fact that so many voters helped to make up the various audiences.

Pittsburgh Press, August 8, 1915

CLINTON COUNTY (August 9–11)

The Woman's Bell Attracts Crowds on Main Street: Arrives Behind Schedule

The suffrage liberty bell has come and gone through the streets of Lockhaven, mute. The Liberty Bell of our country rang and spoke and became mute. This bell we hope will speak for centuries when its tongue is untied after the second of next November, proclaiming to all that women and men are on equal terms of franchise.

The bell was met at the county line by a number of loyal suffragists and escorted to town down the Main Street of which it passed through a crowd of interested people, stopping at the Hotel Irvin for supper.

Miss Emma MacAlarney, state organizer, spoke in her usual fascinating manner to the crowds at the post office, the bell soon appearing and the crowd becoming greater.

Mr. Hippel Makes Plea

Miss MacAlarney was followed by a most illuminating, frank, and open presentment of the cause by our own local orator, Henry Hipple, Esq., who extended the freedom of the city to the bell and ladies. He said the suffrage bell did not convey to him the same message as the Liberty Bell, for the Liberty Bell typified fair play and justice to all, and certainly women were not getting it now.

Grandmothers Out of Date

Mrs. Richard FitzGerald followed. She gave a few practical illustrations of the difference between women now and in their grandmother's day, and what they have accomplished, and what they might do if they were given the vote. Miss Louise Hall spoke more along the lines of civics and suffrage, and of how the women had stood behind Judge Lindsey in his great fight against graft in Denver; of what they had accomplished in Chicago and cleaning up the city's dumping ground, where the mortality in the tenements was higher than that of Constantinople. That has been changed. She also spoke of the inspectors now of both garbage and factories, of the decreased death rate, and more comfortable living conditions, and asked for the vote for more freedom.

The bell and party left today for Lycoming County. A stop was scheduled for the shops at Avis at noon, after which they will be met by the Lycoming County committee and escorted to Jersey Shore. An elaborate program and parade winding up with speech making and a band concert is planned for this evening at Williamsport.

Lockhaven (PA) Express, August 11, 1915

LYCOMING COUNTY (August 11–12)

Visit of Suffrage Bell Will Be Long Remembered in Lycoming County: Yesterday Was Largest "Suffrage Day" in the History of the County—Helen Hoyt Talks with Driver of Car, Which Has Carried Suffrage Bell 2,000 Miles of Its Journey

Yesterday was the largest "suffrage day" in the history of Lycoming County. Everybody turned out to see the suffrage bell: suffragists, as well as those who were not inclined towards suffrage were alike interested in this monstrous bell, which has been patterned after our own glorious liberty bell and which is now making a tour of the state in the effort to secure liberty and freedom for the women; to give them the same privileges that the men have been enjoying ever since the original liberty bell tolled freedom for the United States, July 4, 1776.

In a few moments' talk with Oliver Hall, the driver of the machine which has carried the suffrage bell two thousand miles since the journey began, June 23, in Bradford County, [reporter] Helen Hoyt learned some very interesting points. The party expects to keep right on going through the state, from county to county, until November 2, election day. Mr. Hall is an ardent suffragist and was greatly pleased with the way the bell and the accompanying party were received in Williamsport. "We've had splendid receptions in many places we have visited. In some places, of course, there is more enthusiasm shown than in others, but I think Williamsport has indicated that the sentiments of the people run toward suffrage. If the same interest is manifest in the places we visit, as in those places we have left, there can be no doubt but that there will be victory in 1915." Those are some of the views of the young man who has driven the suffrage bell through two thousand miles of its journey and who expects to drive it seven thousand miles more.

The party has been traveling more than six weeks, and there has been no serious delay. All of the towns have been reached on scheduled time, or nearly so, and the only inconveniences have been blowouts, or some other minor troubles with the machine. "Most of the accidents have very conveniently happened on days which have been kept for "Rest Days" and consequently there has been no trouble." The so-called "Rest Days" must be more or less of a joke with him by this time.

The mayor of Williamsport and numerous city officials were among those who greeted the suffrage bell as it entered the county line. At Newbury, there was a flag stop as Miss Louise Hall, state Secretary of the Woman's Suffrage Association, termed it. Because of the interest that was displayed, Miss Hall had the parade stopped and gave a short, but very interesting talk to the large number of men, women and children who had gathered in Diamond square.

The visit of the suffrage Bell will be remembered in Williamsport and in Lycoming County, and the many who

intended to vote for suffrage in November are doubtlessly just as decided as ever that it is the proper way to vote, and it is hoped that others who did not intend to vote that way have been won over by the splendid speeches and efforts of the women of the Equal Suffrage Association of Pennsylvania.
Daily Gazette and Bulletin (Williamsport, PA), August 12, 1915

SUFFRAGIST SPOTLIGHT

Oliver Hall (1891–1965)

Oliver Hall, 1915.

Oliver Cushing Hall was born on May 29, 1891, in Newport, Rhode Island, to Martin Ellsworth Hall and Mary Cushing Hall. One of four children, he was the younger brother of suffragist Louise Hall.

Hall graduated from the Massachusetts Institute of Technology in 1914 with a degree in electrical engineering, and on May 2 of that year, he served as marshal of the MIT section of a suffrage parade in Boston.[42] Already a committed suffragist, he drove the truck that carried the Justice Bell on its 1915 tour of Pennsylvania and also served as the tour's official photographer.

By 1916, Hall was working for AT&T in the Long Distance Lines Department. He later joined Bell Telephone Laboratories in New York City, where he worked on the development of toll circuits and dial telephone systems.[43] He married Charlotte "Lottie" Curtis on January 13, 1917. His World War I draft card from that year lists the couple living with one child, Lottie's son from a previous marriage.[44] They later divorced.

He married May Frances Gardner on January 2, 1930, in New York City. The couple had four children. Oliver Hall died on December 3, 1965, at the age of seventy-four.

AUGUST 12–AUGUST 23

Sullivan, Bradford, Wyoming, Susquehanna, Wayne, Pike, Monroe

An unidentified speaker addresses a crowd from the back of the truck carrying the Justice Bell, 1915.

Elizabeth McShane and the Justice Bell, Pennsylvania, 1915.

Highlights

The Justice Bell began its journey into the northeastern part of the state on August 12, with its first stops in sparsely populated Sullivan County. A delegation of local suffragists met the bell party at the county line to act as an honor guard, escorting the bell through small towns for rallies where Louise Hall and Emma MacAlarney delivered speeches. The party made a brief stop in the southeastern corner of Bradford County, visiting New Albany and Wyalusing, before continuing to Tunkhannock in Wyoming County for a Saturday night gathering—one of the largest events the town had ever seen. When the bell truck again experienced mechanical trouble, the suffragists used Sunday to rest while the vehicle was serviced. By Monday, they were back on the road, making stops in Factoryville and Nicholson before reaching Susquehanna County on August 16.

Two days later, the truck broke down again, this time in the town of Susquehanna, and required extensive repairs. Hannah Patterson, who had been traveling with the bell in a support role, went to Scranton on August 19 to find a mechanic. Meanwhile, Oliver Hall gave another interview about the tour, this time to the *Carbondale Daily News.*

While the truck was being repaired, the suffragists continued without it, traveling to towns in Wayne and Pike Counties. Although attendees were disappointed by the Justice Bell's absence, large crowds still gathered to hear the speeches. To make up for the missing bell, the suffragists put extra effort into engaging the audiences and raising much-needed funds through the sale of bell souvenirs.

On August 20, the repaired truck rejoined the suffrage caravan as it entered Pike County. They reached southeastern Wayne County the following day, where Louise Hall delivered a speech. That evening, local suffragists escorted the bell back across the county line to Milford, in Pike County. It remained there through Sunday.

On August 23, with the tour finally back on track, the Justice Bell entered Monroe County, where it was greeted by a delegation of local suffragists in automobiles. In Stroudsburg, a mass meeting drew a large crowd to hear speeches by Emma MacAlarney and Adella Potter, an experienced speaker from Brooklyn, New York, who joined the bell party in Monroe County and remained with the group until the end of the tour on October 30.

SULLIVAN COUNTY / BRADFORD COUNTY (August 12–14)

Suffrage Bell Coming

Bearing with it the hearty good wishes of thousands of voters from every county through which it has passed in its history making tour of the state, the Woman's Liberty Bell will arrive in this county on August 12.

The bell, which is being transported on a huge motor truck, will be met at the county line by a delegation of Sullivan suffragist who will act as a guard of honor to it. While it is in this county stops will be made and open air meetings held at the following places:

August 12 – 6 o'clock Eagles Mere
August 13 – 3:45 Laporte
August 13 – 5:30 Dushore
August 14 – Into Bradford County
August 14 – 10:45 New Albany
August 14 – Noon Wyalusing

At these meetings, the women speakers who are accompanying the bell will explain its message.
Sullivan Review (Dushore, PA), August 11, 1915

WYOMING COUNTY (August 14–16)

Suffrage Bell Rests in Tunkhannock: Speakers Urge Votes for Women in Wyoming County Towns

Tunkhannock, Pa., August 16—The Woman's Liberty Bell and its escort were entertained over Sunday in Tunkhannock, and while the machinery of the auto truck was overhauled the speakers rested and made repairs to their nerves.

It was a peaceful Sunday for Tunkhannock after the vigorous Saturday night doings, when the town greeted the Bell and the suffrage campaigners. Last night's meeting was one of the biggest that has ever been held in the streets of this place, and it was regarded by local suffragist as a triumph for their cause.

The bell truck arrived late as it was delayed on the road from Meshoppen [Wyoming County] by half a dozen unexpected demands for speeches, but the crowd was not kept waiting long, for Miss Emma MacAlarney, one of the speakers with the party who had preceded the bell, stepped into an unoccupied auto and held the attention of a restless throng for nearly three-quarters of an hour.

Miss MacAlarney's address had done a whole lot to convert the unconverted of Tunkhannock, and Miss Louise Hall, who arrived with the bell, completed the job. The suffragists have just opened new headquarters in a main street place, which was contributed rent free by Leah Burns, and it was elaborately decorated last night. The suffrage matrons remained at home and were lined up to greet the campaigners, but the younger set which is active in the work here went in search of the bell, and a score of pretty girls accompanied it into town, half a dozen of them riding on the truck.

The party left here today at 10 o'clock. Factoryville will be the first stop. The bell will arrive at Nicholson [Wyoming County] at noon and stop at Hop Bottom Springs [Susquehanna County] on the way to Montrose where the party will remain overnight.

Wilkes-Barre (PA) Times Leader, the Evening News, August 16, 1915

SUSQUEHANNA COUNTY (August 16–19)

Liberty Bell Headed This Way but Stuck in Susquehanna: If Good Luck Prevails Will Get Down This Way as Far as Forest City—Will Then Go to Prompton and Honesdale

Susquehanna, Pa., August 19—The Woman's Liberty Bell party was all day yesterday at Susquehanna for repairs. There is nothing the matter with the suffrage arguments or the suffrage speakers, and the bell is in good condition, but the gray truck is suffering with half a dozen ailments, and it has been necessary to call in a specialist from Philadelphia.

Oliver Hall, the young college graduate and brother of Miss Louise Hall, conductor of the campaign, who is engineer and chauffeur of the party, is responsible for the following diagnosis of the truck's ailments:

"The truck," Mr. Hall said, "has lost one tooth of the rear axle bevel driving pinion. There should be sixteen teeth, and at present the pinion has only fifteen. The radiator cap is gone, but that is a minor ailment. The lower axle bushing lock washer is in bad shape and must be replaced, and one lower axle bushing grease cup is needed. Outside of this, the machine is all right, and when it has been overhauled, which probably will be this morning, we will be able to start on our tour again."

Today the party will visit—if the operations on the ailing truck are successful—Jackson, Ararat, Herrick Center, Uniondale, Forest City, Waymart, Prompton and Honesdale.

Carbondale (PA) Daily News, August 19, 1915

WAYNE COUNTY / PIKE COUNTY (August 18–22)

Bell Party Tours Southern Wayne: Outbursts of Oratory and Applause Along Route: Escort Autos Save Delay

The disabled Liberty Bell truck in a Susquehanna garage and the delayed parts necessary for its repair and operation caused great disappointment along the route where the appearance of the bell was scheduled in southern Wayne County. On Friday, the bell party comprising Miss Louise Hall, Miss Elizabeth McShane, both Vassar college graduates and sent out by the Pennsylvania State Woman Suffrage Association; Miss Rose D. Weston, correspondent for the North American; and the county chairman, Mrs. A. R. Pennell, left Honesdale [Wayne County] at 9:30 for Ariel [Wayne County] where the first stop was made.

As their automobile with its yellow plumes and suffrage banners rolled into town, it was received by a delegation of Boy Scouts, who gave the scout cry and stood at attention when Miss McShane put forth her arguments for the enfranchisement of women. The Scouts who were from the German Presbyterian church in Scranton are camping at Ariel and came of their own accord, which added much to the pleasure and fitness of the occasion. The crowds that gathered were plainly disappointed at the absence of the bell, but gave an attentive hearing to the speaker.

The run into Hamlin was made and the townspeople met the party with hearty welcome. Mrs. Jessie Lyman and Miss Emma May Buckingham presented the speakers with beautiful bouquets of flowers.

At Paupack [Pike County], the people had congregated at the Methodist church and as the car rolled in sight, the ringing of the church bell announced its approach. Here, Miss McShane spoke for fifteen minutes and responded to the active demand for bell souvenirs which she offered for sale.

From here the party motored through historic Tafton [Pike County] crossing the bridge at Wilsonville [Pike County], once the county seat of Wayne and Pike, then into Hawley [Wayne County].

Miss Louise Hall spoke for an hour and twenty minutes to a crowd of several hundred people in front of the bank building and made one of her most telling efforts in this the biggest and best meeting of the whole campaign in Wayne. The bell arrived in Hawley on Saturday [August 21] where it was met and escorted into Milford by Mesdames Van Etten, Wolfe and Eddington of that borough.

Wayne Independent (Honesdale, PA), August 24, 1915

MONROE COUNTY (August 23)

Suffrage Bell Welcomed: Guard of Honor Meets Emblem at Monroe County Line

Stroudsburg, Pa., August 24—Escorted by a delegation of Monroe County suffragists in decorated automobiles, the Suffrage Liberty Bell arrived here late yesterday. The bell was met at the county line by a guard of honor. Upon the arrival of the bell here, adherents of the suffrage cause held a meeting on the courthouse steps, where an address of welcome was made by Judge Staples.

There was a mass meeting in the evening. Miss Emma MacAlarney and Miss Adella Potter, who are touring with the bell, and A. Mitchell Palmer spoke.

Evening Public Ledger (Philadelphia, PA), August 24, 1915

SUFFRAGIST SPOTLIGHT

Adella Emma Potter (1876–1966)

Adella Emma Potter, 1915.

Adella Emma Potter was born on July 8, 1876, in Brooklyn, New York, the second child of Eva Vaunt Potter and Dr. Charles Potter. Her sister, Eva Sherwood Potter, was also active in the suffrage movement.

In 1902, Potter earned a law degree from New York University. A gifted public speaker, she spent the following years traveling widely in support of women's suffrage and was frequently quoted in newspapers.[45]

In 1913, she attended Carrie Chapman Catt's suffrage school and, later that year, rode a white horse as grand marshal of the Brooklyn parade, where the original plaster Justice Bell made its second appearance.

Potter was already a well-known and respected speaker in Pennsylvania when she joined the Justice Bell tour in August 1915. She gave speeches in Monroe County and remained with the bell party through the tour's conclusion, delivering the final speech of the campaign in Chester County on October 30.

Like many suffragists, Potter's activism was shaped by her work in New York's settlement houses, where she came to view the vote as essential to empowering poor women to demand better living conditions. In 1916, she spent several months in West Virginia assisting women in their campaign for a state suffrage amendment, although the measure ultimately failed.

Potter returned to New York and continued her suffrage work. On November 6, 1917, women won the right to vote in New York, making it the first eastern state where men approved a women's suffrage amendment. Afterward, she shifted her focus to the prohibition movement, joining the Anti-Saloon League to advocate for the Eighteenth Amendment.

In 1922, Potter married William M. Potter (no relation), who had two children from a previous marriage. During the 1930s, the family relocated to

New Jersey, where she became active in the League of Women Voters. She later moved to Florida, where she died on October 31, 1966, at the age of ninety.[46]

AUGUST 24–SEPTEMBER 14

Carbon, Lehigh, Northampton, Monroe, Lackawanna, Luzerne

Louise Hall and Elizabeth McShane, co-directors of the Justice Bell tour, 1915.

The Justice Bell in Scranton, Pennsylvania, Justice Bell tour, 1915.

Highlights

By August 24, the suffragists and the Justice Bell had been on the road for two months when they entered Carbon County. Despite the arduous journey, their commitment to the cause never wavered. With more than ten weeks and many miles still ahead before reaching their final destination in Chester County, appreciative crowds buoyed their spirits and strengthened their resolve.

The bell party reached Lehigh County on August 26, drawing crowds that included workers in towns such as Palmerton and Allentown, where industrial plants and factories granted employees time off to attend rallies. To address labor concerns, the PWSA added Rose Winslow and Gertrude Breslau Fuller to its roster of speakers. Winslow, a nationally known former child laborer, joined the tour in late August and remained through September. Fuller, a socialist lawyer from Illinois and a prominent advocate for workers' rights, joined the tour in early September and remained with the group through most of October.

While suffrage organizations worked tirelessly to educate the public and ensure the Justice Bell tour's success, anti-suffrage groups were also well organized and turned out in force. The Pennsylvania Association Opposed to Woman Suffrage, led by Deborah Norris Coleman Brock of Lebanon, wielded significant influence, as did leaders in the coal and textile industries. Despite their efforts, the Justice Bell continued to draw large crowds.

On August 28, when the bell party reached Bath in Northampton County, a town known for its strong anti-suffrage sentiment, a crowd of several hundred gathered to see the bell and hear Adella Potter and Katharine Ruschenberger deliver speeches.

The Justice Bell arrived in Monroe County on September 1, welcomed by Philadelphia's mayor, Rudolph Blankenburg, and his wife, Lucretia Blankenburg, both longtime advocates for women's suffrage. Over the next three days, the bell made numerous stops at boarding houses and summer hotels.

On September 4, the bell party entered Lackawanna County, a hub of iron production and the anthracite coal industry, for a week-long visit. Kate Chapman (Mrs. Maxwell Chapman), chair of the Lackawanna County division of the PWSA, had meticulously planned an itinerary that brought the bell to towns across the county, beginning with its appearance as a main attraction in Scranton's Labor Day parade.

With just over seven weeks remaining until the election, the Justice Bell entered Luzerne County on September 11. For four days, the suffragists traveled through towns along the Wyoming Valley, leading parades and delivering speeches at mass rallies. They reached Wilkes-Barre on September 14, the final stop on this leg of the journey.

CARBON COUNTY (August 24–26)

> ***Woman's Suffrage Bell***
>
> The Woman's Suffrage Bell has come and gone. From its entrance into Carbon on Tuesday afternoon [August 24] to the last stop at Palmerton early on Friday afternoon [August 27], it has made stops with meetings and speeches at several places. The most notable gatherings were at Mauch Chunk, Summit Hill, Lansford, Nesquehoning, Weatherly and Lehighton. At the meeting at Leighton last week, the attendance was estimated at fully two thousand.
>
> A surprising interest and enthusiasm were shown everywhere and the fact that Carbon County has the unique distinction of a visit from Mrs. Ruschenberger, the donor of the bell, who came to Mauch Chunk, and was entertained by Judge and Mrs. Barber, added much to the character of the occasion. The carefully planned schedule was maintained everywhere without the slightest mishap, although at the dangerous turn on the hill road between Summit Hill and Lansford, the big truck carrying the bell nearly escaped going over the edge and down the mountain side.
>
> The committee accompanying the bell have been most pleased with all the plans made by the Carbon organization and have stated that the arrangements in this county have been the most satisfactory of any county thus far visited.
>
> The bell was formally handed over to the Lehigh County committee at Slatington today.
>
> *Mauch Chunk (PA) Times-News*, August 30, 1915

LEHIGH COUNTY (August 26–28)

Suffragists Plead Cause Before Crowd of 1500 on Centre Square: City and County Have No Organization of Votes-for-Women Workers; No Reception Committee Met the Bell on Its Arrival Here

Allentown paid her respects to the Woman's Liberty Bell, which is making a tour of the state in the interest of women suffrage, and which it is expected, will be rung for the first time in Independence Square in November, following the election, announcing to the world that women have been given the vote in this state. Wherever the bell has been, it has been received with a great show of interest and the meetings attending its arrival have been enthusiastic and attended by a large number of the representative voters.

These conditions were repeated in this city last night, when the trophy arrived on its specially constructed automobile and was viewed by hundreds while in front of the American Hotel, the headquarters of the attending committee, and later at the Square where a monster meeting was held. It was estimated that there were about 1500 present, who listened to the addresses on the growth and worth of the granting of equal franchise to women.

The speakers were Miss Emma MacAlarney, of New York, and Miss Elizabeth McShane, of Uniontown, both forceful and convincing speakers who thoroughly explained the cause for which they are striving. Miss MacAlarney in her remarks stated that Allentown, though not organized, was practicing the principles of the equal rights of the sexes and illustrated the point by referring to the new women's college, nurses' home, high school, and Deaconess Home, with other apt references of what the city was doing along the lines of giving all equal opportunities.

The emblem arrived on schedule time, 5:15, after a triumphal trip of the county, with the last stop being at Siegersville. It was displayed on the Square and later at Sixth and Hamilton Sts., while its escort of suffrage workers were dining at the American Hotel. Hundreds at these points viewed the novel display.

Each one was delighted with the city and expressed the hope and confidence that Lehigh County would be heard from in the coming election.

Allentown (PA) Democrat, August 28, 1915

SUFFRAGIST SPOTLIGHT

Rose Winslow (1889–1934)

Rose Winslow (Ruza Wenclawska), 1916.

Rose Winslow was born Ruza Wenclawska on December 15, 1889, in Suwałki, Poland, one of eleven children. Her parents, John and Blanche Winslow, immigrated to the United States in 1890.

At age eleven, Winslow began working in a Philadelphia hosiery factory. After developing tuberculosis around age eighteen, she spent time in a sanitarium. She later became a powerful advocate for workers' rights, including protections for child laborers.

Following a speech she delivered at a fundraiser for tuberculosis relief, the Philadelphia Consumers' League hired her as a factory inspector. By 1910, she was a full-time labor activist. In 1913, she became a member of the Women's Trade Union League and worked as a speaker and organizer for the Women's Political Union, a New York-based suffrage organization founded by Harriot Stanton Blatch. The Congressional Union for Woman Suffrage (later the National Woman's Party) hired her as an organizer in 1914.[47]

Before joining the Justice Bell tour, Winslow delivered a series of speeches in Lawrence County, Pennsylvania, in mid-August 1915. A local newspaper, the *New Castle Herald*, praised her abilities: "When the bill for a 54-hour work week for women was under consideration, her speech before the Pennsylvania State Legislature did much to secure its passage. To secure other laws for the protection of women and children, Miss Winslow believes that women suffrage is a necessity. She is devoting to this campaign the eloquence which is hers, seemingly as a special gift for her work, and has become one of the most able advocates of votes for women."[48]

Winslow joined the Justice Bell tour in late August and September 1915, speaking in Lackawanna, Luzerne, Lehigh, Monroe, and Northampton Counties. Known as the "factory girl suffragist," she viewed women's suffrage as essential to protecting the rights of women and children.

In 1916, when the famous suffragist Inez Milholland collapsed and died in Los Angeles while delivering a speech during a tour for the National Woman's Party, Winslow took her place, giving speeches in Arizona. In 1917, Winslow joined the picketers at the White House in Washington, DC, and was arrested, incarcerated, and force-fed after joining the suffragists on a hunger strike.

Winslow later had a moderately successful acting career in New York. She spent her final years as a patient in the tuberculosis ward at Central Islip State Hospital in New York, where she died on April 16, 1934, at the age of forty-four.[49]

NORTHAMPTON COUNTY (August 28–September 1)

The Woman Suffrage Bell in Bath

The [Woman's] Liberty Bell, which was presented by Mrs. Charles W. Ruschenberger, of Philadelphia, is an exact replica of the original Liberty Bell. In a three-thousand-mile itinerary through the state on an auto truck, it reached Bath on Saturday at 4 o'clock from Bethlehem. There was an escort of six young ladies of town dressed in Suffrage colors—yellow—accompanying the two large autos with the State and County Officers and the scheduled speakers. The procession halted on "The Square" where the meeting was held. Several hundred people were in attendance. The addresses made by Miss Eva Potter, New York City, and Mrs. Charles W. Ruschenberger were exceptionally fine and illuminating.

Hitherto the sentiment antagonistic to Woman Suffrage prevailed in Bath, but nearly every intelligent person realizes the cause will carry victory eventually in spite of the pros and cons.

Morning Call (Allentown, PA), September 1, 1915

MONROE COUNTY (September 1–4)

Bell in Poconos: Greeted by Throngs, Mayor and Mrs. Blankenburg and Mrs. Staples

Mayor and Mrs. Blankenburg set the suffrage example Wednesday at Mount Pocono, and both came out, she officially as one of the oldest members of the state organization, to welcome the woman's liberty bell. Mrs. Blankenburg arranged and managed a series of meetings in the Poconos, which began Wednesday afternoon [September 1] with a porch gathering at the Pocono Pines Assembly and which terminated at night with a big meeting held at the home of Dr. Anna P. Sharpless of Philadelphia, at the Pocono Manor.

One of the most enthusiastic meetings of the day and the one which gathered together the greatest number of voters was held at the Mount Pocono railway station in the afternoon.

Here, the townspeople, travelers, hikers, automobilists, station workers, baggage handlers, and storekeepers flocked to see the bell, which had been widely heralded in this section, owing to the vast work done by Miss Lida Stokes Adams of Philadelphia and a group of lively workers. Here, Miss Rose Winslow delivered an address which men said was the "straight from the shoulder" kind, and the women agreed was the right kind for the men to hear.

The bell was accompanied to the station by Mrs. Blankenburg and a delegation of Pocono workers, and here, with the freight trains halting to take on and let off passengers, Miss Winslow spoke for almost half an hour. The crowd was loath to see her go when the party started out for the Manor where the night meeting was held.

While the meeting was in progress, the mayor came over from the Blankenburg bungalow, across the road, and quietly and unofficially looked at the bell. The mayor has not been making engagements this summer and for this reason he did not deliver an address, but Mrs. Blankenburg who had been affiliated with the movement for years, spoke a few words in introducing the speakers. The coming of the bell suspended business when it drove into sight.

The party started out the next morning under the escort of Mrs. Charles Staple, wife of Judge Staple of Stroudsburg, the capable and indefatigable county chairman. The bell made numerous stops at the big boarding houses, and the summer hotels that make the Poconos the playground of this part of the country. Stops were made at Paradise Valley, Cresco Mountain House, and Buck Hill Falls.

Wayne Independent (Honesdale, PA), September 7, 1915

SUFFRAGIST SPOTLIGHT

Lucretia Blankenburg (1845–1937)

Lucretia Longshore Blankenburg, 1914.

Lucretia Mott Longshore was born on May 8, 1845, on a farm near Lisbon, Ohio, to Thomas Ellwood Longshore, a schoolteacher, and Hannah E. Myers Longshore. Named for her mother's friend, suffragist and abolitionist Lucretia Mott, she was a second-generation suffragist. Soon after her birth, the family moved to Bucks County, Pennsylvania, and in 1850 relocated to Philadelphia so Hannah could attend the Woman's Medical College of Pennsylvania, from which she graduated in 1851.

Lucretia married Rudolph Blankenburg, a young German immigrant, in a Quaker ceremony on April 18, 1867. He was elected mayor of Philadelphia in 1911 and served a four-year term. The Blankenburgs had three children, all of whom died young. Later, they raised a niece and a nephew.

In 1878, Lucretia Blankenburg joined the recently founded New Century Club, which, she later wrote, "deepened [her] interest in public affairs." As part of her social activism, she was instrumental in appointing women to leadership positions. In the early 1880s, she helped Eliza Sproat Turner organize the New Century Guild, a club for working women, and also taught evening classes there.[50]

Blankenburg served as president of the Pennsylvania Woman Suffrage Association (PWSA) from 1892 to 1908 and remained active in the movement afterward. She and her husband welcomed the bell party when it arrived in Mount Pocono, Monroe County, on September 1, 1915. Lucretia had arranged a series of meetings and events over a three-day period for the Justice Bell and the traveling suffragists as they passed through the county.

Lucretia Blankenburg died on March 29, 1937, at the age of ninety-two.

LACKAWANNA COUNTY (September 4–11)

Great Enthusiasm Greets Liberty Bell on Tour: Meetings at Dunmore, Throop, Olyphant and Other Points Up the Valley: Rally at Carbondale: Held Last Night and Drew Big Crowd—Where the Bell Will Go Today

With its mute appeal to give liberty to the women of Pennsylvania in that they may have the right to vote, the Woman's Liberty Bell, escorted by prominent suffrage leaders of the country and members of the Lackawanna County Suffrage Party, toured the mid-valley and Dunmore yesterday. The final meeting today was held at Carbondale, following which the bell and truck was quartered at a garage there, while the speakers returned to this city.

It was a most successful tour, Miss Elizabeth McShane, of Uniontown, PA, director general of the bell tour declaring that "the interest manifested by the people of Lackawanna County in our fight to secure the ballot, was highly encouraging."

The members of the party yesterday included: Mr. and Mrs. Maxwell Chapman, Mrs. Chapman [Kate Chapman] is chairman of the local county suffrage party; Miss Dorothy Walls, Lewisburg; Oliver Hall, driver of the bell truck, Harrisburg; Mrs. Walter McNab Miller [Helen Guthrie Miller], president of the suffrage association of Missouri, first auditor of the national suffrage association, and member of the trades union league of Missouri; Miss Rose Winslow, New York; Miss Rose Weston, Philadelphia ... and Mrs. Gertrude Fuller of Pittsburgh.

Told Story of the Bell

Probably the most interested in the Liberty Bell were the children along the route, and at the towns where meetings were held. At the conclusion of every street session, Miss McShane, who is a graduate of Vassar College, gathered the children around her and undertook to explain to them the story of the national relic, of which the suffrage bell is an exact replica.

These meetings were the most interesting. Mrs. Fuller and several of the other speakers would expound at length upon the reasons why they should be given the ballot, and then the grownups would move back and the children would gather around the bell while Miss McShane in simple phrases told them the story of the bell, which on July 4, 1776, proclaimed liberty throughout the country.

Little breaker boys [child coal miners], their faces black and grimy, linked hand in hand with school children, listened attentively while the story of the bell was unfolded to them. Their eyes sparkled with pleasure as Miss McShane smiled upon them and in her motherly and simple way told them of the hardships our forefathers went through in their struggle to gain independence.

Wherever the bell truck halted, were it for a few minutes on the roadside or in one of the towns at which the party was scheduled to speak, the children were the most interested. They would climb up on the truck, and with a feeling of awe, touch the sides of the great bell. This done, Jimmy or Mary would shout "I touched it," while mothers standing on the edge of the crowd looked on and smiled.

The Tribune (Scranton, PA), September 8, 1915

SUFFRAGIST SPOTLIGHT

Kate Chapman (1865–1937)

Undated photograph of Kate Chapman.

Kate Chapman was born Kate Amelia Ryon on August 10, 1865, in Elkland, Pennsylvania, the youngest of three children of Charles Ryon and Sylvina Gertrude Hoyt Ryon. On December 9, 1886, she married Maxwell Chapman, a civil engineer from Port Blanchard. The couple had one child. By 1900, they had moved to Dunmore, a suburb of Scranton, where Kate lived for the rest of her life.[51]

In 1913, as suffragists worked to secure the votes needed for the Pennsylvania legislature to pass the state suffrage amendment, Chapman was called upon by Jennie Bradley Roessing to obtain a key endorsement from the Central Labor Union of Scranton.[52] The following year, she played a leading role in the movement while serving in multiple positions: as chair of the Lackawanna County division, a vice president of the Pennsylvania Woman Suffrage Association (PWSA), and the founder and president of the Lackawanna County Equal Suffrage League. Among her many contributions, she oversaw the 46th Annual Convention of the PWSA, held at the Hotel Casey in Scranton in November 1914.[53]

Chapman was active in the Justice Bell campaign. She attended the sendoff of the Justice Bell in Sayre on June 23, 1915, delivered speeches in Bradford County, and was the primary organizer of Scranton's 1915 Labor Day parade, where the bell was prominently featured. In 1920, she was among those who traveled to Philadelphia to hear the Justice Bell ring for the first time.[54]

In 1921, Chapman made history as the first woman to run for elected office in Lackawanna County. She won the nomination for county treasurer on the Prohibition ticket but was narrowly defeated in the general election.[55]

Kate Chapman died on July 10, 1937, at the age of seventy-five.

LUZERNE COUNTY (September 11–14)

> ***Stirring Scenes as New Liberty Bell Tours the Valley***
>
> All of the leaders of the suffrage movement who accompanied the touring party, expressed themselves as well pleased with the hearty reception accorded them and their liberty bell as it started its tour of Luzerne County. The bell was received from the Lackawanna delegation at the county line in upper Duryea at four o'clock yesterday afternoon. Duryea's demonstration was one of the finest that any small town has accorded the party. Four hundred school children were in the parade that received the bell and there were liberal decorations of American colors on the homes and business places.
>
> There was also a brief stop at upper Pittston. Miss Rose Winslow had been expected to speak there, but Mrs. Maxwell Chapman, of Scranton, took her place and gave a brief address that evoked considerable applause. The procession then resumed the trip down Main Street and made a halt at the Eagle Hotel, where the party were entertained at dinner and where the Liberty Bell rested until the evening meeting, receiving much attention from the people who gathered.
>
> Escorted by a squad of mounted state police, a score of

automobiles gaily decorated in the party colors and a number of enthusiastic workers, the Pennsylvania Suffrage Liberty Bell resumed its tour through the Wyoming Valley at 9 o'clock this morning and arrived at Wilkes-Barre at noon after a most successful morning campaigning. Everywhere along the line, the bell was greeted by the plaudits of the men as well as the cheers of enthusiastic women and from all outward indications, the voters of the Wyoming Valley will stand staunchly by the first amendment on the ballot at the November election and Woman Suffrage will be given substantial support in this region.
Pittston (PA) Gazette, September 11, 1915

SEPTEMBER 14–SEPTEMBER 27

Columbia, Montour, Northumberland, Union, Snyder, Juniata

Elizabeth McShane with the Justice Bell, 1915.

Highlights

Despite unusually hot weather that soared into the upper 90s, a crowd that included one thousand children, hundreds of suffragists, and the Berwick Band, greeted the bell party as the Luzerne County delegation handed the Justice Bell over to Columbia County suffragists. Over the next two weeks, the bell party traveled through several less-populated counties, yet each drew hundreds to roadside meetings and even larger crowds to city gatherings. Schools had allowed the children to attend parades, and factories had released their workers early so they could see the bell. Mary Bakewell, who had joined the bell party in Luzerne County and was serving as vice president of the PWSA, inspired local residents with her speeches as she described the mission of the Justice Bell—to establish equality for women—and the hoped-for outcome of the November 2 election.

Between September 16 and 22, the bell party traveled back and forth through three counties: Montour, Union, and Northumberland. On September 16, the Justice Bell entered Montour County, making multiple stops in rural communities but avoiding Danville, where the State Department of Health had banned all public events due to a typhoid fever outbreak.[56] Instead, the bell party traveled to Exchange, where more than one hundred residents gathered to hear Elizabeth McShane, one of the tour's most popular speakers. McShane now shared tour director duties with Louise Hall and also oversaw fundraising for the campaign. Souvenirs made of the same metal as the bell—pins, watch fobs, and bracelets—were especially popular.

In Union County, the escort party included local resident and Justice Bell tour speaker Dr. Mary Wolfe. In Northumberland County, the bell's arrival was marked by a parade of fifteen hundred people. Local suffrage leaders, who had spent weeks organizing the events, now took center stage, including Maida T. Strecker, president of the Northumberland County Woman Suffrage Association, who welcomed the bell party with a speech.

The following day, still in Northumberland County, the Justice Bell was welcomed with parades and large crowds in towns including Allenwood and Sunbury, where Mary Bakewell and Elizabeth McShane delivered speeches. On September 20, the bell party traveled to Mifflinburg in Union County, where houses were decorated with yellow banners and a parade featured floats adorned in patriotic colors.

From September 23 to 27, the suffragists traveled through the final two counties of this leg of the tour. In Selinsgrove, Snyder County, children marched behind the bell truck as it rolled into town. More than a thousand people gathered to hear speeches by Adella Potter and Gertrude Breslau Fuller, both of whom urged the crowd to stand firm in their commitment to securing the vote for women. The bell's arrival in Juniata County was met with similar enthusiasm. In Mifflintown, the suffragists stayed until Monday, rallying local support before continuing to Thompsontown and Millerstown and crossing into Perry County.

COLUMBIA COUNTY (September 14–15)

Suffragists Pay Act of Courtesy to an Invalid: Liberty Bell Taken Out of Its Route that She Might View the Emblem: Millville Made the Bell's Reception a Gala Event and Turned Out Well

It was a pretty act of courtesy those in charge of the suffrage liberty bell paid an invalid near Rohrsburg yesterday. She had expressed a wish that she might see the bell that typified the cause for which she stood, and off the prescribed route the bell was taken that her heart's desire might be gratified.

Altogether, it was a big day as the night before in Benton had been. The start from Benton for Rohrsburg was made at 9:30 o'clock, and all along the way farmers came from their fields to greet the bell and receive suffrage literature, and the school children were out to witness the passing of the emblem of equal rights for women.

Rohrsburg turned out in full force to receive the bell and there Miss Bakewell spoke. There, also, the Millville suffragists met the party and accompanied them on their way into Millville. All along the approach to Millville, suffrage flags on the trees greeted the party and nearly every porch in Millville had a huge jardinière of yellow flowers. Lunch was had there at noon and the meeting, an exceptionally large one, was held at 12:45 o'clock, with Miss Bakewell introduced by Miss Myra Eves.

From there, the party went to Jerseytown, where there was another good meeting, and then to Exchange and Washingtonville, where the Montour and Northumberland County suffragists took charge.

Mrs. S. J. Houk [Katherine Terwilliger Houk], the county president, and Mrs. J. W. Bruner accompanied the party throughout the day.
Morning Press (Bloomsburg, PA), September 17, 1915

MONTOUR COUNTY / NORTHUMBERLAND COUNTY (September 16–18)

Woman's Liberty Bell in Montour: School Children Meet Bell

Neither the excessively hot weather nor the very dusty roads failed to dim the ardor of the Woman's Liberty Bell party that toured the northern part of Montour County yesterday.

The bell was viewed by hundreds in Montour County, after the big bell truck had entered Montour from Columbia County. The last stop in Columbia was at Jerseytown, and the first stop in Montour was at Exchange. From Exchange the party proceeded to Washingtonville where another brief stop was made. From Washingtonville, the bell party went to Milton [Northumberland County] where last night was spent.

This morning the bell will retrace its steps into Montour County. The schedule as printed in the *News* yesterday will be adhered to. Mausdale and Mooresburg will be visited as well as Mooresburg, the time at the former place being 2:30 p.m. and at the latter place, 3:15.

The bell, mounted on its big motor truck, attracted much attention as it passed over the country roads in this county yesterday afternoon. All along the route, farm houses displayed goldenrod and other yellow flowers, and farmers came running from the fields to see the emblem pass by.

At Exchange a demonstration that particularly pleased the bell party was held. The bell was met by 38 school children led by their teacher, John Yagle. A crowd of over a hundred people at this place listened to Miss Elizabeth McShane expound the woman suffrage doctrines.

In the bell party were Oliver Hall, driver of the truck, a brother of Miss Louise Hall, a prominent Pennsylvania suffragist; Miss Mary Bakewell of Pittsburgh, vice president of the state suffrage association; [and] Miss Elizabeth McShane, of Uniontown. Miss Dorothy Walls, of Lewisburg, and Miss Florence Shimer,

of Milton, are with the party temporarily as aides. Another interesting member of the bell party was Miss Rose Weston, of the *Philadelphia North American* staff, whose suffrage and other articles in that newspaper have attracted wide attention.
Danville (PA) News, September 17, 1915

SUFFRAGIST SPOTLIGHT

Mary Bakewell (1868–1960)

Undated photograph of Mary Bakewell.

Mary Ellen "Ella" Bakewell was born on July 5, 1868, to Ellen Frances Boardman Bakewell and Benjamin Bakewell, whose family was prominent in the glass-making industry. She was the eldest of three daughters.[57]

Although best known for her suffrage work, Bakewell also advocated for children as a member of the International Kindergarten Union and the Allegheny and Pittsburgh Free Kindergarten Association.

In 1904, Bakewell co-founded the Allegheny County Equal Rights Association (ACERA), later renamed the Equal Franchise Federation of Western Pennsylvania. She served first as its secretary and later as its president. In 1912, she was elected Western Vice President of the Pennsylvania Woman Suffrage Association (PWSA) in a pivotal election that shifted power from suffragists in the eastern part of the state to those in the western counties, including Jennie Bradley Roessing, Hannah Patterson, and Lucy Kennedy Miller, all from Pittsburgh.

In 1914, Mary Bakewell and Lucy Kennedy Miller established the School for Suffrage Workers, where University of Pittsburgh faculty taught more than one hundred women courses on government, constitutional law, the legal status of women, taxation, and public speaking. Bakewell was a principal speaker during September and October of the Justice Bell tour, when the party traveled through the state's eastern and southern counties.

In 1917, Bakewell, then first vice chair of the National Woman's Party (NWP), joined fellow members Alice Paul, Lucy Burns, and hundreds of others in picketing in front of the White House in Washington, DC, urging Congress to pass a federal amendment granting women the right to vote. The protesters, known as the Silent Sentinels because they didn't speak, held banners calling on President Wilson to support women's suffrage.

At age fifty, Bakewell enrolled at the Hartford Theological Seminary to become an Episcopal minister. However, shortly after moving to Wyoming to lead a parish, she left the church and returned to Pennsylvania to pursue other interests.

In her later years, Bakewell returned to her love of writing. Having published two books for children in 1901 and 1902,[58] she authored two more in 1949: *Of Long Ago: The Children and the City* (University of Pittsburgh Press) and *What Woman Is Here?: The Autobiography of a Woman Pioneer in the Rural West* (Oxford University Press).

Mary Bakewell died on May 31, 1960, at the age of ninety-one.

NORTHUMBERLAND COUNTY (September 17)

Woman's Liberty Bell: Will Be in Town Next Monday Afternoon

The bell entered Northumberland County at Mooresburg this Friday afternoon and was met by a delegation of leading county suffragists, who will act as a guard of honor to it while in the county. Tonight, the bell will be in Milton where a big parade and mass meeting is to be held. Fire companies and other organizations of that town will participate in the parade. Tomorrow the bell will be taken through the upper end of the county and a portion of Union County. In the evening, it will be at Lewisburg where there is to be a big celebration.

Sunday will be spent in Lewisburg, and on Monday after the tour of Union County has been completed, the bell will be brought to Northumberland.

From this place, the bell will be taken to Sunbury, where Monday evening will be spent. Sunbury suffragists have planned an elaborate celebration for the occasion. There will be a parade and an open air meeting starting at 7:30. Many Northumberland people will likely go to Sunbury for the evening events.

The tour of Northumberland County takes in most of the towns and hamlets. It will culminate at Selinsgrove next

Thursday night [September 23].
Public Press (Northumberland, PA), September 17, 1915

UNION COUNTY / NORTHUMBERLAND COUNTY (September 18–22)

Suffrage Bell Given Big Reception Here

Union County had the great pleasure Saturday of receiving the Suffrage Liberty Bell, which has been making a tour of all the counties in the state.

The Bell arrived on time at Allenwood at the northern end of our county that afternoon. Most of the houses were decorated in the Suffrage colors and the population was out on the streets looking for the Bell and eager to hear the speeches. Miss Mary Bakewell, of Pittsburgh, spoke, as also did Prof. T. F. Hamblin, of Bucknell University. Dr. Hamblin made one of the best speeches for the cause of Suffrage anyone has ever had the pleasure of hearing. Allenwood was most cordial in its reception of the Bell and as it came time to leave, one cheer after another went forth from the crowd as the whole party pulled out for the next town.

A great pleasure and a big surprise awaited the party at New Columbia. When the truck on which rested the big bell pulled into New Columbia, the school children, all dressed in white with yellow sashes, met the party and surrounded the Bell. The whole town was out to welcome the Bell and its party. Miss McShane, who manages the Bell tour, spoke here. Miss McShane is from Uniontown and her talk was one of the best of the afternoon. For one so young, Miss McShane certainly knows what she is talking about when speaking for suffrage. She explained the significance of the bell and did it in such a manner that the older people, as well as the children, were delighted.

One thing which pleased everyone was the fact that along the country roads the rural school buildings were decorated and the scholars dismissed long enough for all pupils to see the bell.

The party was due back in Mifflinburg at 12:30 p.m. The bell party was met at the extreme end of town by a section of the Citizens band of Lewisburg. The Boy Scouts acted as an escort for the bell. The school girls, dressed in white and yellow, marched in back of the bell. At least thirty automobiles were in line beautifully decorated. All along the line of the parade, the business places and residences were tastefully decorated in yellow. One beautiful float in red, white and blue carried the Goddess of Liberty. The headquarters for the whole party was the famous Buffalo Valley Inn, where speeches were made. Miss Louise Hall, who has swung many votes for the amendment the last few weeks, was the first speaker introduced. Then Miss Bakewell was introduced and when she concluded her talk, she received hearty applause.

Thus, one will see that all through Union County the Woman's Liberty Bell and its party were well received. Nowhere did they lack a welcome and those with the bell had good things to say of Union County.

Lewisburg (PA) Journal, September 24, 1915

SNYDER COUNTY (September 23–25)

Town and Country Ready for Suffrage Bell Campaigners: Public Meeting in Square Tonight

Snyder county suffragists will go to Shamokin Dam this afternoon to greet the women's liberty bell as it comes across the river bridge into the political arena.

County workers have decided to make memorable the visit of the bell to this section, and have left nothing undone for that accomplishment from the time the "bellers" reach Snyder County at 10 am until they motor into Juniata County Saturday afternoon after spending two nights in this thrifty agricultural and industrial community.

The speakers on the tour through Snyder County will be Miss Adella Potter, of Brooklyn, N.Y., and Miss Gertrude B. Fuller, of Pittsburgh. They will be presented by Mrs. Schroyer.

Yellow daisies, fluffy pompons, suffrage pennants, and other suffrage emblems will flash and glow from residences, business houses, and automobiles this afternoon. Those who are going to Shamokin Dam to meet the Bell when it enters the county, will leave town about 4:30 p.m. Of course, the county leader will lead the possession.

The local suffrage workers will assemble in the square at 7:15 o'clock in order to have everything in readiness for the opening of the evening meeting, which will start promptly on the arrival of the speakers. The suffrage aides for the meeting are Mrs. Irvin

Romig, Miss Lisle Foster, Miss Margaret Foster, Miss Potteiger, Mrs. Eyer and Mrs. Heffelfinger.

Come and hear the suffrage cause presented by experts. If anyone cares to ask any question in regard to the cause, the speakers will be glad to hear them and answer them at the close of the meeting.

Selinsgrove (PA) Times-Tribune, September 23, 1915

SUFFRAGIST SPOTLIGHT

Gertrude Breslau Fuller (1870–1952)

Gertrude Breslau Fuller, 1902.

Gertrude Blanche Breslau was born on December 10, 1870, in Chicago, Illinois, the daughter of James Cushman Breslau, a war artist and correspondent for the *New York Tribune*, who died when she was an infant. Her mother, Melissa M. Darrall Breslau, was a well-known Shakespearean actress. When she was five years old, Henry H. Kaiser and Diadma Best Kaiser kidnapped her and took her to Iowa, where they raised her. She was not reunited with her mother until she was twenty.[59]

Over the years, Breslau was known by several last names—Davies, Hunt, Deininger, and Fuller—each reflecting one of her four marriages. On October 6, 1912, she married Albert M. Fuller and was thereafter known as Gertrude Breslau Fuller.

Breslau practiced law in Chicago, but over time she became disillusioned with the court system, telling a reporter in 1904, "I soon learned that the courts are simply a strainer. They sift out the small fry, who usually get nothing for lack of funds to carry cases up. That conviction led me to a study of economic justice. I am now finishing up my last cases, and will devote all the energy of heart, body and soul to pointing the way to industrial freedom for all classes."[60]

True to her word, Breslau dedicated the rest of her life to advocating for workers, women, and children. She became an author and leading writer for the Socialist Party. She joined the Justice Bell tour as a speaker in early September 1915 in Lackawanna County and remained with it through most of October, giving her final speech in Montgomery County.

As a socialist, she largely focused on labor issues, particularly the importance of women receiving equal pay for equal work. As reported on September 23, 1915, by the *Mount Carmel Item* in Northumberland County: "Mrs. Gertrude Breslau Fuller . . . told of how in 75 of the great industries of the state, women work side-by-side with the men but only receive half as much pay. The women must pay the full price for everything they buy, however. 'If women had the vote, they could make a fight for better wages. The men higher up, however, are opposed to women suffrage because they don't want them to have the weapon, the vote to help themselves,' she said. 'Some people say that the women would not know how to vote. The trouble is the big boys know that they would know how to vote to get liberty and justice and that they fear the outcome.' . . . She stated that the greatest opposition to suffrage comes from those who don't want the working people to have the vote so that they can't better their conditions."

By 1920, Fuller was living in Pittsburgh. In 1921, after she had joined the Democratic Party, the Socialist Party presented the Democratic Party of Berks County with a framed photograph of her that had been in their possession.[61] She continued to support the Democratic Party in various capacities and remained a political force through her writing and public speaking.

Fuller was hospitalized in May 1949 at a tuberculosis hospital in Pittsburgh and died there on November 20, 1952, at the age of eighty-two.[62]

JUNIATA COUNTY (September 25–27)

> ***Suffrage Bell at Thompsontown***
>
> *Thompsontown, Pa., Sept 28*—The woman's Liberty Bell accompanied by the Misses Potter, McShane and MacAlarney, together with the county officers, received a splendid ovation in the public square. At 2:30 o'clock, the school children scattered beautiful yellow dahlias and zinnias over the bell as they marched past the truck. Miss Emma L. MacAlarney, the speaker, was introduced by the Rev. D. B. Treibley. After a half hour's address, the party proceeded to Millerstown, Newport and New Bloomfield.
>
> *Harrisburg (PA) Telegraph*, September 29, 1915

SEPTEMBER 27–OCTOBER 9

Perry, Dauphin, Cumberland, Franklin, Fulton, Adams, York

A speaker, most likely Mary Bakewell with Jennie Bradley Roessing standing below, addresses a crowd while passing through Carlisle, Pennsylvania, October 1, 1915.

Highlights

The tour through the southern counties brought the Justice Bell and suffragists to more populated areas. Some of the most moving speeches took place on the grounds at Gettysburg, in Adams County, and some of the largest crowds gathered at the York County Fair.

By this time, newspapers across the country—and nearly all local papers—were reporting on the bell's journey, offering detailed coverage of the suffragists, their speeches, and often exhaustive lists of local supporters. With so much publicity, towns sought to make a strong impression. Decorated automobiles escorted the bell into communities to the sound of marching bands. Shop windows overflowed with yellow flowers, children wore suffrage sashes, and supporters staged elaborate receptions.

From September 27 to 28, the Justice Bell drew large crowds in Perry County, where Emma MacAlarney and Adella Potter were the featured speakers. In Harrisburg, Dauphin County, a crowd of two thousand greeted the bell with cheers and music.

The bell party entered Cumberland County on October 1 with a new driver behind the wheel. Oliver Hall had left the tour after the Harrisburg events, and Frank Roessing, the husband of Jennie Bradley Roessing, assumed the driving duties. In Carlisle, Ethel Vorce, secretary of the Ohio Woman's Suffrage Association, joined speakers Dr. Mary Wolfe and Mary Bakewell as they continued to draw large crowds.

In Chambersburg, in Franklin County, the welcome included a bugler, women on horseback, and a bicycle squad. College students and town residents alike turned out across the region, braving the return of bad weather in some towns. In McConnellsburg, the only stop in Fulton County, more than fifty automobiles escorted the bell into town as church bells rang out, and nearly two thousand people gathered to hear the message.

On October 5, representatives of the Gettysburg Club met the Justice Bell in Fairfield, in Adams County, and escorted it to the grounds of the Civil War battle at Gettysburg, where Ethel Vorce and Mary Bakewell delivered speeches.

The bell party spent five days in York County, where months of planning had gone into a full schedule of events, with Anna D. Gamble, president of the county chapter of the PWSA, at the helm. Over five thousand people turned out in York on October 5, and the bell's appearance at the county fair two days later drew thousands more. As the party prepared to leave the county, they made a final stop in Shrewsbury to honor the heartfelt request of Mary H. Eberhart, who was too ill to attend the rally. The suffragists brought the bell to her bedroom window so she could recite her poem, "Columbia's Daughters," in its honor.[63]

With Election Day, November 2, less than one month away, the suffragists had nine counties remaining before reaching West Chester, the final stop of the tour. Large, enthusiastic crowds throughout the campaign had persuaded the weary travelers that the men of Pennsylvania would support the women of the state and grant them the right to vote.

PERRY COUNTY (September 27–28)

> ***Woman's Liberty Bell in Perry County***
>
> Bearing with it the hearty good wishes of thousands of voters from every county through which it has passed in its history-making tour of the state, the Woman's Liberty Bell will arrive in this county on September 27, 1915.
>
> The bell, which is being transported on a huge motor truck, will be met at the county line by a delegation of Perry suffragists, who will act as a guard of honor to it while in this county.
>
> At the meetings, the women speakers who are accompanying the bell will explain its message and ask the help of the men of Perry County to unfasten the chains which hold the great bronze tongue of the bell silent. The men's help is needed because the chains are not to be removed from the bell until the women of Pennsylvania are granted the right to vote. It is within the man's power to say just when that day shall be.
>
> The women are hopeful that it will be November second of this year when, for the first time in the history of Pennsylvania, a suffrage amendment to the State Constitution will be voted upon. They base this hope not only upon the spirit of fair play, which governs the great majority of men of Pennsylvania, but upon the tremendous enthusiasm which the big bronze symbol of their appeal for political independence has aroused in every town it has visited.
>
> In virtually every one of these towns, the crowds that have turned out to see the bell and hear the suffrage speeches have been bigger than those ever assembled for outdoor rallies of any

sort in the past. Moreover, according to the newspaper reports along the route, the crowds have been more than enthusiastic. They have paid the suffragists the compliment of listening attentively to every argument advanced for giving women the ballot, and in many towns, hundreds of men have voluntarily pledged themselves to vote for the suffrage amendment in November.

The speakers who will accompany the bell through this county are Miss Emma L. MacAlarney and Miss Adella Potter.

Perry County Times (New Bloomfield, PA), September 23, 1915

DAUPHIN COUNTY (September 28–30)

Women's Emblem Continues Tour: Bell Is Welcomed in Regal Style by Suffragists

Continuing its triumphal tour of the county, the suffrage liberty bell today invaded Hummelstown, Hershey, Highspire, and Steelton. At each stop it was met by large delegations of suffragists who received the speakers with wild enthusiasm. The bell will return to the city tonight after a rally at Steelton.

Harrisburg welcomed the bell in royal style last evening. It was met at Front and Division streets by scores of suffragists and automobiles decorated with Votes for Women signs and gay yellow streamers. The machines fell in line in back of the truck bearing the bell, and headed by the municipal band, traversed many of the principal streets of the city before falling out in Market Square.

Fully 2,000 persons, the majority men, packed about the truck in Market Square last evening to hear the speakers plead for votes for the suffrage amendment. Mrs. John Oenslager presided and introduced Miss Emma L. MacAlarney of this city, and Miss Adella Potter, of Brooklyn.

Miss MacAlarney, after reminding the city of the progress made in the last fifteen years, said that Harrisburg owes much of its advancement to its women. She reminded the men that the club women have ever been in the forefront in carrying out and instigating improvements and that they virtually initiated the movement for a better and more beautiful city.

The speaker concluded by telling that these same women who have been responsible for much of the civic advancement were

asking for a share in its government and in the government of the State and she asked if any men in the crowd would question their right to it.
Harrisburg (PA) Telegraph, September 30, 1915

CUMBERLAND COUNTY (October 1–2)

Carlisle Sees the Liberty Bell and Hears "Suffs" Speak: Heavy Rain Fails to Dampen Enthusiasm. Truck Goes Hub-Deep in Mud Along Roads; Starts on Journey up the Valley

Rain scarcely dampened the enthusiasm of Carlisle's welcome to the Suffrage Liberty Bell which, in charge of its fair adherents, arrived here at 4 o'clock from Harrisburg and was here for the night, leaving this morning on a continuation of the journey up the valley.

Following is the story of the liberty bell's visit as related by a newspaper woman traveling with the bell [Rose Weston, reporter for the *North American*].

It didn't make a bit of difference to Carlisle. The rain tumbled down, the trees dripped and waterspouts spouted, and the road disappeared beneath the puddles.

Carlisle wanted to see the woman's liberty bell, and it saw it. It saw it from beneath its beautiful old colonial doorways; it saw it from the shelter of umbrellas and from behind its many-paned windows. But it saw it, and it took a long look; and it liked it so well that tonight the town square, which looks like a town lake, is jammed with rain-coated individuals who want another look.

Carlisle's reception to the new liberty bell came as one of the big surprises of the suffrage campaign. All day the party had gone on in a driving storm, with only two epochs of relief to mark the day—one at noon at Mechanicsburg, when the townsfolk came out and warmed and encouraged the hearts of the drenched speakers by their unswerving attention to an address delivered from the shelter of a big umbrella, and the other at New Kingston, when a group of kindly and warm hearted folk lined up beneath the awning of the general store and gave the bell and its escort three cheers.

Occasionally, a small boy would dash out and yell "votes for women," "see the Liberty Bell," and then things would subside.

And the bell would go on, accompanied by the slush of the water as it drove hub deep in the rivulets of the road, and by the steady slap of the raindrops on the roof of the truck.

The delegation of Carlisle women who met the party as it came across the river and entered Cumberland County never lost heart, and the big yellow banners on the backs of their cars acted as beckoning flames to the truck.

Yellow Banners Blaze Trail

The delegation of Carlisle women who met the party as it came across the river and entered Cumberland County never lost heart, and the big yellow banners on the backs of their cars acted as beckoning flames to the truck.

Miss Mary Norcross, the county leader, whose cheering presence was a joy throughout the entire day, told the campaigners that the Carlisle preparations which had been made and perfected for weeks in advance had been wrecked completely by the rain. "We will just go into town and leave the bell at the garage," Miss Norcross said, and the delegation of autos leading the bell slowed up rather mournfully. Then the streets suddenly seemed to fill with umbrellas. One wild-eyed urchin spread the news, and in a minute every doorway held all the occupants of the house who could cluster in it. The youngsters defied the weather and came out. One dear old woman grabbed a huge "votes for women" flag and waved it from her doorstep.

Business men left their offices and stepped to the curb. "Hurrah for suffrage. Good for you. We are not fair-weather friends. We will give you our vote," they shouted. Soon the town had caught the infection and everyone was waving and shouting and the bell was getting the reception of its three months career. *Carlisle (PA) Evening Herald*, October 2, 1915.

SUFFRAGIST SPOTLIGHT

Ethel Ridgley Vorce (1876–1963)

Ethel Ridgley Vorce, 1915.

Ethel Caroline Ridgley was born on May 1, 1876, in Detroit, Michigan, the daughter of Robert Bruce Ridgley and Caroline Mellen Ridgely. In 1896, she married Albyn V. D. Stearns, who died suddenly later that year. In 1903, she moved to Cleveland, Ohio, where she married her second husband, Myron Bond Vorce. They had no children.

Ethel Vorce became a leader in the women's suffrage movement, serving as secretary of the Ohio Woman's Suffrage Association and as the first organizer and later as vice chair of the Woman Suffrage Party of Cuyahoga County. In 1912, she attended the International Woman Suffrage Congress in Budapest and then traveled to London, where she attended more suffrage meetings. In 1915, she represented Ohio at several national suffrage conventions.[64]

Vorce joined the Justice Bell tour as a speaker in October 1915, delivering speeches in Cumberland, Fulton, Franklin, Adams, York, and Lancaster Counties. The *Lancaster New Era* reported on her speech on October 11, 1915: "Mrs. Vorce kept her audience in great good humor by her rapid-fire stories, in the telling of which she is a past master. She interspersed the stories with logical arguments in favor of equal suffrage, showing that it has not 'unsexed' the women of the West; that the men and women in those states marry and rear families, just the same as everywhere; that they can find a place to put their babies while they cast their ballots just as well as when they go to pay their taxes. She insisted that the women of Pennsylvania will never give up the fight for suffrage, and that the men had better save themselves expense by granting them their wish at the next election."

After returning to Detroit in 1917 or 1918, Vorce continued her suffrage work as a member of the Equal Suffrage League of Wayne County. After ratification of the Nineteenth Amendment, Vorce, like many suffragists, turned her attention to teaching women about their newfound power. In

1920, she was elected vice president of the Michigan League of Women Voters.

After the Nineteenth Amendment was ratified, Vorce remained active in numerous social causes, serving in leadership positions for a variety of organizations. She joined the Detroit branch of the Women's International League for Peace and Freedom in 1924 and later served as vice president. In 1921, Vorce was elected president of the Michigan branch of the Women's Committee on World Disarmament. In 1931, she was elected vice chair of the Michigan branch of the Women's Organization for National Prohibition Reform, an organization which had been founded in 1929 to repeal the Eighteenth Amendment. In 1935, she was elected fourth vice chair of the Michigan Division of the Women's Organization for Non-Partisan Reforms.

Ethel Vorce remained active in civic and political affairs throughout her later years. She died on May 18, 1963, at the age of eighty-seven.

FRANKLIN COUNTY (October 2–4)

> ***Equal Suffrage Party Makes Triumphant Tour Across Franklin County: The Bell Brigae Invades Cumberland Valley, is Enthusiastically Welcomed, and its Orators are Given Attentive Hearing***
>
> The Cumberland Valley was invaded on Saturday last, stops being made at all the principal points along the line, the party and the bell arriving in Chambersburg about 5 o'clock, being met at the outskirts of the borough by a large delegation of citizens, including Burgess Wingerd. Many prominent men, mounted on horses and wearing yellow sashes acted as marshals, while a long string of automobiles was occupied by men and women, many of the cars being gaily decorated with the colors of the suffrage party. A couple of ponies attached to carts, in which children sat, were also an attractive feature of the pageant. Another big feature of the parade was the reception given by Wilson College and Penn Hall students, who gathered on the campus, mingling their college yell with "votes for women."
>
> A large crowd lined the route of the procession through town, being given liberal applause; while those among the body of spectators who had not yet been convinced that votes should be given to women, looked on and wondered.

In the evening, a fairly large size crowd assembled in front of the Central Presbyterian church, where stood the bell on its truck, to hear what the fair advocates of "Votes for Women" had to say.

On Monday, the tour of the county was begun in a westerly direction, the bell being accompanied on his journey by several local members of the Suffrage party.

The first step was made at St. Thomas where a large crowd had assembled to greet the bell. The speaker, Dr. Mary Wolfe, the most eloquent of them all.

On top of the mountain at Tuscarora, the party was met by ten automobiles and fifty citizens from McConnellsburg. A procession was formed and a parade was given through the streets of McConnellsburg. When the party entered the town, all the church bells and the courthouse bell rang out a welcome.

The last stop was made at Waynesboro where the Quincy Orphanage Band, Mrs. Fisher, Mrs. Lowe, Mrs. Criswell and Mrs. Defoe of the Waynesboro organization, and many citizens in automobiles. A procession was formed which paraded through the town and at 8 o'clock speeches were given by Mrs. Vorce and Dr. Wolfe, who were introduced by the Rev. Franklin Boggs. The addresses were heard with perfect attention by a crowd of fully a thousand people, made up mostly of men.

In speaking of the tour, a leading suffragist just told a *Register* man that the journey was eminently successful from any standpoint, and anyone connected with the movement was highly gratified, believing that success will be theirs on November 2.

People's Register (Chambersburg, PA), October 7, 1915

FULTON COUNTY (October 4)

Woman's Liberty Bell: Bronze Model of the Original Liberty Bell Attracts Thousands; Sincere Women Plead for Rights

As announced, the Woman's Liberty Bell was exhibited in McConnellsburg on Monday. More than fifty people in automobiles met the party, who traveled with the bell at the county line on Cove Mountain, and escorted it to town. When the party came in sight, all the church bells in town were rung as if in greeting to their sister visitors. Soon nearly 2,000 pairs of eyes were looking eagerly for a first sight of the already famous replica of the old Liberty Bell of revolutionary fame. A lone rider, Miss Harriet Sloan, on a handsome bay, marshaled a short parade in town, after which the huge truck was stopped at the stone wall at L. W. Seylar's drug store, and Mr. Seylar, in a very appropriate address, introduced the accompanying speakers, Mrs. Vorce and Mrs. Dr. Wolfe who presented convincing arguments that with present day modes of living come demands on women's work that were unknown in the days of our forefathers. For woman to fill the sphere allotted to her in present times, she must have equal rights at the polls with men. They presented word pictures of conditions in cities not realized by us country people. We, therefore, who represent but one third of the population of this county, should not forget the two-thirds who depend upon agriculturists for food and who, regardless of sex, that individually struggle for existence.

A matter worthy of note is the nonpartisan spirit of this woman's campaign. The women are fighting for principle—not for any party. The clean, dignified, efficient manner in which the local women handled Monday's convention is but a reflection of the ability that is backing the work in the State. Can the men voters show greater executive ability?

Fulton County News (McConnellsburg, PA), October 7, 1915

ADAMS COUNTY (October 5–6)

Liberty Bell's Trip to Adams County: Women Orators Make Plea for Share of Government "By the People and For the People"

The woman's liberty bell and corps of speakers have passed through Adams County. The trip was made on Tuesday and Wednesday and certainly was one of education. The able speakers readily answered all questions in an indisputable way, and presented most logical conclusions as to why they should have thc ballot.

The following account is from the pen of Miss Rose D. Weston, a special representative of *The North American*, who is accompanying the bell on its trip throughout the state:

Lincoln's words, spoken on the battlefield of Gettysburg;

Lincoln's appeal for a government "of the people, for the people, by the people," and his utterance, "I go for all sharing the responsibilities of government, by no means excluding women," were spoken Tuesday within a stone's throw of the battlefield by women who are seeking their share, as people, in that government.

The woman's liberty bell, which is to proclaim justice and the full establishment of liberty when the women of Pennsylvania are enfranchised, was carried Tuesday over the hallowed hills of Gettysburg. With its yellow banners crying their insistent demand for votes for women, with its silent tongue protesting by its muteness against women's enslavement by the old political order of things, the bell entered Gettysburg.

Along the government highways that have been dedicated forever to the immortal struggle, past Willoughby's run, along Seminary Avenue, past Lee's headquarters, on into town over the route made sacred by memorable sacrifices, the women carried their symbol of freedom.

In the crowd that greeted the bell in the town Square were scores of negroes, men and women, some of them old enough to have been born in slavery.

The nearness of the battlefield, the echo of Lincoln's great address, the surging associations of the war, and the thought of the principle which it was fought to establish, came over the women who are waging a peaceful fight for their liberty. They entered the town in a reverent and a sober spirit, and in the addresses delivered by their two speakers, Mrs. Myron Vorce, of Cleveland, Ohio, and Miss Mary E Bakewell, of Pittsburgh, there was an echo of this spirit.

"I stand here in the name of American womanhood," Mrs. Vorce said, as she mounted the platform at the end of the truck, "asking not that you men shed your blood for us to make good the principle which was established on this battlefield, but that you use that symbol of freedom, your vote, to confer equality on us. To the right and the left of us and all about these fields, are monuments to those who died to free an enslaved race.

"We women are asking today that you put us on a political basis with the men then freed. We want you to make Lincoln's words a living truth. We are people, one-half the people, and until you enfranchise us this will be a government of the people, for the people, BY THE MEN. We do not want to do your work or take your places. We are not going to quarrel with you or to antagonize you. We simply want our share in the government under which we live."

Both speakers reminded the men who gathered in the Square that the matter of suffrage must be settled in the state of Pennsylvania at the polls on November 2, but they reminded them also that if it is not settled favorably, it simply will be deferred, and that the decision against suffrage will mean the opening of a new campaign to gain it.

Veteran's Dollar for 'Ballot'

In the crowd were many Grand Army veterans. One came forward with tears in his eyes and handed the speaker a dollar. "I believe in liberty for all," he said, "and I am for you women."

At the gates of the cemetery, two old men with their little bronze buttons in the lapels of their coats, came out and asked for souvenirs of the bell. They were Union soldiers, from Maine, revisiting the scene of the great battle, and glad to see the bell and learn of its mission.

Through a chilling rain the bell campaigners traveled until they came to their noonday stop at Fairfield. The school children stood in an awed little procession in front of the bell and sang "America." "Our Father's God, to Thee, Author of Liberty," they sang, and as their voices rose clear and sweet, the sun broke through the clouds and the shadows of dancing leaves wavered across the bell.

Adams County Independent (Littlestown, PA), October 8, 1915

YORK COUNTY (October 5–9)

Pleas for Suffrage Before Great Crowd Seeing Liberty Bell: More Than 5,000 Persons Viewed Replica of Historic Bell Here—Enthusiastic Meeting in Front of Court House

"Help break the chains that hold the bronze clapper silent by voting 'Yes' on the Suffrage amendment on November 2 next," is the message in brief brought by the Woman's Liberty Bell and its party of attractive speakers to York last evening at a rousing open air meeting in front of the court house.

It is estimated that more than 5,000 persons viewed the bell and listened to the speeches between 8 and 10 o'clock. So dense was the crowd that it was impossible for street cars to run and automobiles were completely stalled as the people surged to and fro between Duke Street and the square. That there was a fine interest aroused, there is no doubt. Attorney Robert C. Blair was the presiding officer of the evening.

Short Street Parade

A short street parade preceded the meeting in front of the court house. The bell was parked in front of the Central school building, West King Street, during the supper hour. From this point, the marchers moved to Beaver street, north to Market and east to the place of meeting. The City Band of York with Prof. John Denues directing, furnished the music. A pleasing incident in connection with the rendition of the music was the fact that the band several times played John Philip Sousa's well known march "The Liberty Bell."

Miss Bakewell was the first speaker of the evening. Of all the suffrage speakers Yorkers have heard since the movement has gained such wonderful ground in this vicinity, it is believed Miss Bakewell is one of the most satisfactory all around speakers. Her clear tones and earnest manner go a long way in convincing many to the cause who now may be members of the anti's camp. Her arguments, too, indicate that she has threshed out the question pretty thoroughly, and that she is sure the work will never lag, is evidenced in her assertion: "If you don't grant us with the vote next November, we will be back at you again next year just as hard as we are today."

Mrs. Vorce told the audience that a good many people are of the opinion that politics is no place for a woman. "Knowing that the woman is well qualified as a housekeeper, just you turn loose the lot of them that you have here in Pennsylvania and see how soon we will clean things up. If politics are too corrupt for women, it is too corrupt for men."

Will Help Name President

Dr. Wolfe presented the importance of the votes of the already enfranchised women in the United States. She sounded a warning that the female vote would also have a lot to do with the selecting of the next candidate for the presidency.

The concluding speeches of the evening were made by Prof. A.A. Holden, principal of the York High School and attorney

Charles A. Hawkins, of Delta. Both were liberally applauded.

The bell, which is stirring up this great enthusiasm throughout Pennsylvania, is practically a replica of the original Liberty Bell, now on exhibition at the Panama-Pacific exposition in San Francisco. It is the same size and the same weight, 2,000 pounds. The only difference is that the crack in the old one has not been duplicated in the new one. The clause "establish justice" has also been added to the inscription, "Proclaim Liberty Throughout the Land to all the Inhabitants Thereof."

The Gazette (York, PA), October 7, 1915

OCTOBER 9–OCTOBER 30

Lancaster, Lebanon, Lancaster (second visit), Berks, Montgomery, Bucks, Montgomery (second visit), Philadelphia, Delaware, Chester

Suffragists with the Justice Bell in Lebanon, Pennsylvania, October 11, 1915.

Suffragists with the Justice Bell in Lebanon, Pennsylvania, October 11, 1915.

Highlights

With only three weeks remaining in the campaign, the Justice Bell entered some of Pennsylvania's most populous counties. In Lancaster, several thousand lined the streets on October 9 for a lively parade of decorated cars and a procession of over a thousand marchers. Interest in the speakers was so great that organizers held two simultaneous meetings to accommodate the crowds.

In Lebanon County, the bell was met with enthusiasm, despite the area being home to Deborah Norris Coleman Brock, president of the Pennsylvania Association Opposed to Woman Suffrage. Antoinette Funk, a lawyer from Illinois, joined the tour to speak in Lebanon, Berks, and Montgomery Counties. On October 12, the PWSA dispatched Louise Hall and Elizabeth McShane to Philadelphia to assist Mary Ingham of the Equal Franchise Society of Philadelphia in the final days leading up to the election.

The bell party returned to Lancaster County for additional rallies on October 12, including one in Ephrata hosted by the Women's Christian Temperance Union (WCTU). In Berks County, the bell drew large crowds to a rally in Reading. The following evening, the party entered Montgomery County for an event before spending the night in Pennsburg.

Momentum continued in Bucks County on October 16, when Helen C. Clark, secretary of the PWSA, assumed the role of tour director. Over the course of two days, the bell visited thirteen towns and drew large audiences. The goodwill carried into the final leg of the journey in Montgomery County, although the reception in Lansdale and Montgomeryville was noticeably cooler. Nevertheless, the speakers pressed on with impassioned speeches about how the vote would benefit both women and men.

Antoinette Funk, Gertrude Breslau Fuller, Dr. Mary Wolfe, and Adella Potter were the key speakers as the bell party made its way through the region. The bell arrived in Conshohocken on October 21, and the following day continued through the towns of the Main Line, traveling in a convoy of decorated automobiles. In Ardmore, Mary Jenkins Ensign, publisher of the *Ardmore Chronicle*, presented a laurel wreath to Rebecca Chapman Winsor, a local suffrage leader, to place on the bell. The wreath was a gift from Winsor's three daughters—Ellen, Mary, and Rebecca Winsor—who were also active in the suffrage movement.

Later that day, the Justice Bell crossed into Philadelphia at Overbrook Station, escorted by officials from multiple suffrage organizations. That evening, the bell was the centerpiece of the Festival of Light, the city's first nighttime suffrage parade. Eight thousand marchers, representing various professions, unions, and suffrage groups, processed down Broad Street in a torchlight parade, with the Justice Bell riding on a flower-covered float pulled by women in flowing white dresses.

On October 25, the bell arrived in Delaware County and was ceremonially handed over to local suffrage officials at the historic Blue Bell Inn. Towns along the route turned out in large numbers, particularly Lansdowne, where the Pennsylvania Men's League for Woman Suffrage played a prominent role. Alice Bedford, chair of the Delaware County Suffrage Party, delivered many of the speeches, with Helen Todd joining her to highlight the progress women had made in California, her home state. The county's tour concluded with an energetic evening event in Wayne.

On October 28, just days before the election, the Justice Bell entered Chester County and was handed over to local suffragists in Berwyn. The final stop occurred on October 30 in West Chester, where the bell was greeted by a large crowd in front of the courthouse. Katharine Ruschenberger reflected on the bell's journey and its symbolic return to the town where Pennsylvania's first women's suffrage meeting had been held in 1852. Adella Potter delivered the tour's final speech, sharing a message of hope and equality. After more than four months on the road, the tour of the Justice Bell—one of the most significant and unique campaigns for women's suffrage—came to an end.

LANCASTER COUNTY (October 9–10)

Reception for Woman Suffrage Bell Elates the Local Supporters: Great Throng Lines Curbs While Big Pageant in Yellow-Bedecked Autos Passes in Review

Lancaster had the greatest equal suffrage demonstration in its history on Saturday [October 9] when the Woman Suffrage Liberty Bell, now completing its celebrated tour of Pennsylvania, passed through the northwestern section of Lancaster County, and in the evening was the center of attraction in a street parade with mass meetings in the county-seat. The parade was of no mean proportions, and both it and the double open air mass meetings, with speakers at two places on Orange Street, were highly successful.

The flying squadron with the bell arrived in the city at six o'clock. While the speakers had dinner at the Stevens House, the auto bearing the new emblem of the "Votes for Women" campaign stood at the main entrance to the hotel on South Prince Street. Hundreds of persons stopped in passing to look at it, and a continuous stream of people were going back and forth from West King Street to examine the much talked about relic. Indeed, it was continually surrounded by a group of curious, interested folk during the entire hour and a-half it stood there. Needless to say, a great many of these were women and girls.

There were also thousands of the fair sex among the great throngs of people who lined the curbs on both sides of the street in the business section of town, and as they waited for and watched the procession of their bolder sisters they talked together in groups, expressing their opinion of the cause and telling each other what they would do if they ever got the vote.
Lancaster (PA) New Era, October 11, 1915

LEBANON COUNTY (October 11–12)

Suffrage Bell Goes to Lebanon County

The Woman's Liberty Bell received an enthusiastic welcome in Lebanon County on Monday. The ladies accompanying the bell left Lancaster in the morning, accompanied by a delegation of members of the local Suffrage Association in an automobile decorated in the color of the Cause. At Manheim, the tourists stopped for an hour, being received by a fair-sized crowd, and here Dr. Mary Wolfe made an address. At Bismarck, the tourists were met by Lebanon County suffragists and Palmyra, Annville and Lebanon were visited.

In the evening, a big meeting was held in Lebanon after a parade, the feature of which was two hundred boys and girls carrying suffragist banners and singing. The mass meeting was presided over by Dr. Warren F. Klein, and Mrs. Antoinette Funk, of Chicago, was the principal speaker.

Mrs. Funk declared that she had always found anti-suffrage leaders numbered among the wealthy, whose incomes can be traced to the product of the laboring class. Mrs. Funk told her audience that the wage question in Pennsylvania will only be satisfactorily solved when the women get suffrage.
Lancaster (PA) New Era, October 12, 1915

SUFFRAGIST SPOTLIGHT

Antoinette Leland Funk (1869–1941)

Antoinette Funk, ca. 1915.

Marie Antoinette Leland was born on May 30, 1873, in Dwight, Illinois. Her parents, Cyrus Leland and Virginia Antoinette Bouverain Leland, died when she was young, and she was raised by her grandfather. She married John Waltrus in 1887, and they had one child. Three years after Waltrus's death, in 1893, she married again—this time to Isaac Lincoln "Linc" Funk, with whom she had one child.[65]

Funk graduated from Illinois Wesleyan University in 1898 and was admitted to the Illinois State Bar Association that same year, becoming one of the first women lawyers in the state. In 1913, she was part of a group of women credited with securing passage of legislation that allowed Illinois women to vote in presidential elections. In 1914, she became chair of the National American Woman Suffrage Association (NAWSA).

Antoinette Funk joined the Justice Bell tour in October 1915, speaking in Lebanon, Berks, and Montgomery Counties. By then, she was a nationally known suffragist, having traveled in numerous states advocating for women's rights and often connecting labor issues with women's suffrage. The *Reading Times* reported a part of the speech Funk gave in Reading on October 14, 1915:

I am going to discuss the labor question, for to me it seems the most vital thing on the republic. One out of every three women is in the bread line, earning her own living in Pennsylvania. The industrial era, the era of machinery is in its zenith. It has taken women out of the home and put them to work, not for themselves, but for someone else. It is the era of exploitation. A class that lives and works in a land whose laws it has no voice, is an exploited class. As a result of exploiting labor, you will hear the men complaining that women are taking their jobs, cutting their wages. And it's true, because you will always find this the case when there is exploited labor because the women are compelled to do a dollar's worth of work for less than a dollar.

They have no way by which they can assert their rights. So you see justice works automatically. It lies within your power, men, to vote against this measure, to compete against your women, but in doing it, you are cutting your own wages, and losing your own jobs.[66]

In addition to her suffrage work, Funk served as a vice chair of the Woman's National Liberty Loan Committee and from 1917–1919, traveled across the country selling Liberty Bonds to help support the US war effort.

After the Nineteenth Amendment passed in 1920, she remained committed to women's rights and continued to travel throughout the United States, making numerous speeches advocating for women and children. From 1933 to 1939, Funk served as the Assistant Commissioner of Public Lands, General Land Office, the first woman to hold that position.

Antoinette Funk died on March 26, 1942, at the age of sixty-eight.[67]

LEBANON COUNTY / LANCASTER COUNTY (October 12–14)

Suffrage Bell Is Again in County: Received Rousing Demonstrations Throughout Lebanon County Tour

Lancaster County again became host to the Woman's Liberty Bell on its state tour in the campaign for the cause of equal suffrage, upon its arrival at Brickerville this morning, from its visit to Lebanon County.

The bell and party were met at Lebanon with a rousing welcome, despite the fact that that place is the home of Mrs. Horace Brock, president of the anti-suffrage organization. A tremendous crowd gathered for one of the largest demonstrations ever witnessed in the city, and the bell party was loudly applauded on every side. The party was escorted to the city by a parade, headed by Tyrell's Band and several troops of Boy Scouts, together with a delegation of more than sixty women. More than five hundred school children walked along in the line of the march. The meeting was addressed by Mrs. Antoinette Funk, of Chicago, executive vice-chairman of the national congressional committee, who made statements which will linger long in the minds of her hearers.

The bell met with enthusiastic welcomes throughout the

entire county and good meetings were held at Bismarck, Palmyra and Annville.

The bell then continued its tour, stopping at Neffsville, Mechanicsburg, Leola, and New Holland, where a meeting will be held this evening, for which elaborate preparations have been made.

On Wednesday, the bell will reach Blue Ball at 10:30 o'clock; Ephrata at 12:15; Denver, 3; Adamstown, 4; and Reading at 6 o'clock, at which place the Berks County organization will take charge.

Intelligencer Journal (Lancaster, PA), October 12, 1915

BERKS COUNTY (October 14–15)

Suffragists Here Over Yellow Path to Obtain Votes: Liberty Bell Center of Admiring Throng in Penn Street Parade: Women Argue Rights

Marching along the dusty road, swinging his pail with one hand and unfolding a blue and pink suffrage folder with the other, many a surprised man strolled home from his work on Wednesday evening with the circular crying "votes for women" in his hands and its contents fermenting in his brain.

The woman's liberty bell arrived from Lancaster Wednesday afternoon. It included Dr. Mary Wolfe, Miss Adella Potter, Charles Heaslip, Miss Rose Weston, and Mrs. Herr [Mary B. Herr], chairman of the association in Lancaster County. They reached Adamstown at 4 o'clock and they were welcomed by a delegation of the Reading suffrage party headed by Mrs. Charles Habel, the president.

Strew Yellow Flowers

School children, mothers and fathers, stopped their work to greet the bell party with the greatest enthusiasm. [Dressed in] yellow, hands flower filled, they strewed the path of the travel wearied but undaunted suffragists with cheer. They sang songs by the wayside and, in response, listened most attentively to the splendid addresses, brief and to the point delivered by professor Mary Wolfe.

Professor Wolfe Address

"When people say, woman's place is in the home, I ask them what they really mean by that. If they think that her world is within the four actual walls, I say no. But if they mean that her place in the home is to help make the home better, I answer yes. But my friends, remember, the home is the center, but not the circumference of all interest.

"Just as the first liberty bell rang out freedom for all men, so this second bell is to proclaim the equality of women. Until then it will be tongue-tied. The women of the west have had the vote for many years, and they have proved themselves fully capable. Do you men of the east find your women so utterly inferior to those of the west. If so, why did you marry them?"

The Reading delegation, in decorated automobiles, followed the truck to Shillington, where Miss Adella Potter addressed the crowds. She urged them to trust their women. She represented home as the bulwark of civilization. Every boost of the home interest added a notch to civilization.

Speeches in Reading

At 7:30 in the evening, the suffragists gathered at Second and Penn Streets to proceed as an escort of the bell to the City Park, countermarching to the Colonial Trust Company building, where Mrs. Antoinette Funk of Chicago was introduced by Mrs. Amanda Woodward Ringler of Reading, and delivered a scintillating address.

Reading (PA) Times, October 14, 1915

BERKS COUNTY and MONTGOMERY COUNTY (October 15–16)

Suffrage Bell in Montgomery on Way Despite Rain: Friedensburg, Yellow House and Boyertown Welcome Women: Sets Men Thinking: Liberty Truck in Front of Cigar Factory, Speaker Talks to Windows

Pennsburg, PA, Oct. 15—Through rain and mud, the woman's liberty bell came into the northern part of Montgomery County.

Crossing the border line between Berks and Montgomery Counties, the bell was escorted to the night meeting place at Pennsburg by Mrs. J. Howard Brown [Martha Nyce Brown], the county chairman, and a delegation of young suffrage enthusiasts from East Greenville. It was a bad day for yellow bunting and paper plumes though the rain remained accommodatingly at bay until after a big noon day meeting had been held at Boyertown, in Berks County, and while the addresses were being made in the Square at Pennsburg last night, it came down in torrents in the afternoon.

Kept to Schedule

But the campaigners have made an inexorable rule not to postpone a meeting or cut out a stopping place on account of the weather, and they have kept faithfully to their schedule through the rain and heat and mud and the adverse weather conditions of the summer. So when clouds broke and the rain came down, they simply hauled in their yellow flags, furled the red, white, and blue, let down the flaps of the auto truck, and went along the road like gypsies in a caravan.

It was fortunate that not many pedestrians were on the road between Boyertown and Hereford, for the women couldn't resist the old impulse to toss out literature and to ask for votes.

School Children Get Liberty

At Friedensburg [later renamed Oley], the first meeting place, the high and elementary schools were dismissed and teachers, pupils and townsfolk gathered on the lawn in front of the school building. Rev. A. H. Schuler and his wife, who had heard of the bell's coming, joined the reception committee, and the minister introduced the speaker, Miss Adella Potter, who appealed to the patriotism of the men in the crowd and to their pride in Pennsylvania, begging them not to let this state remain a laggard in the race of progress. The meeting was under the direction of Miss Mary Stabe and Miss Anna R. Geiss.

Boyertown's Welcome

Boyertown didn't need any second invitation to come out to welcome the bell party. Big yellow announcements, giving the date of the arrival of the new symbol of justice, had been posted in store windows, and they were all that the borough needed to remind it of the event. A big crowd gathered outside the Union House, and while one speaker went inside for lunch, another talked until the factory whistles blew for the return from lunch. Hundreds of employees of the town's industries were disappointed because they were forced to leave without hearing the gist of the suffrage arguments, but later the bell was driven down to the Eisenlohr cigar factory, and the 500 employees came to the windows and stood on the balconies, while Miss Potter outlined to them the principles of the suffrage movement.

Passing through Clayton and Bally, the truck took the road to Hereford, and arrived before the hotel, where a few men were gathered on the porch. It was a small crowd, and somehow it did not seem like a promising one. There was a tendency to hold aloof, and the women felt that there was no warm sentiment in Hereford. But Miss Potter stepped out of the truck in the rain, went up on the porch with the men and talked to them for fifteen minutes. There was a complete transformation in their faces and their attitude, and in a few minutes every man was fumbling for change to toss in the collection basket.

"That was one of the best meetings we have had today," Dr. Mary Wolf, director of the tour, said, as the women waved their farewell to the little knot of men.

"That was as effective as the work of a dozen organizations, for we set those men to thinking as they never had thought before. They are fair minded men; they showed that in their changed attitude. So we can look for at least a few votes from Hereford on election day."

At Yellow House

Yellow House, so called from the big yellow hotel that guards the entrance to the triangular village, gave the bell a curious inspection. Ducks, chickens, geese, dogs and cats evinced a laudable curiosity and mingled with the gatherers at the town pump.

Members of the bell party were guests of Dr. O. S. Kriebel, principle of Perkiomen Seminary, Friday, which is to be a rest day at the seminary.

This morning at chapel, Miss Potter addressed the students, whose interest in suffrage has been aroused by the work of a bevy of pretty workers including Miss E. Herbein, Miss E. Neschter, Miss M. Herbein and Miss F. Shelly.

The Montgomery County tour, which will be taken up again on Monday after the party has left Bucks County, will be under the direction of Mrs. J. Howard Brown, of Ardmore, county chairman, who has formed an effective organization, with headquarters at Norristown.

Reading (PA) Times, October 16, 1915

BUCKS COUNTY (October 16–18)

Bristol Is Ignored; Women Are Indignant: Suffrage Bell Will Not Come to Metropolis of Bucks; Goes to 11 Other Places

Those women in Bristol, who are working for the cause of equal votes, it is said, are somewhat disgruntled, because of the fact that, although the so-called Woman's Liberty Bell has been exhibited in nearly every borough or city of any size in the state, it will not come to this place.

An elaborate program has been arranged for the appearance of the bell in Bucks County, but Bristol has been ignored in the arrangements. It will enter the county at 11 o'clock on the morning of Saturday, October 16, making its first appearance at Quakertown. From there, it will go to Doylestown, stopping at Sellersville, Fountainville and Dublin. After spending Sunday at the county seat, on Monday the bell will be taken to Buckingham, Wrightstown, Newtown, Langhorne, Oakford, and Feasterville. Thence it will go to Montgomery County. Although it will have been shown in eleven places in this county, Bristol, the metropolis, will be utterly ignored. So, it has been asked, haven't the women here got a perfectly good grievance against the managers of the party?

It is announced by the suffrage press agent, that a street meeting will be held here on Friday, October 22. Mrs. Shepherd will be the speaker.

Bristol (PA) Daily Courier, October 6, 1915

MONTGOMERY COUNTY (October 18–22)

Suffrage Bell Heartily Greeted: Bell Was Heartily Escorted into Town by Burgess and a Number of Auto Parties: Gertrude Fuller Spoke

The Liberty Bell of the Woman's Suffrage party arrived here yesterday afternoon at five o'clock and was given a warm and hearty reception.

The bell, a metal one and a replica of the historic Liberty Bell, was mounted on an auto truck, which was decorated with flags and yellow emblems of the suffragists. The bell was followed by a touring car in which was the campaign party. This party came from Norristown by way of Ridge and Conshohocken pikes and was met at Harmonville by Burgess Bloomhall and a number of persons in automobiles.

In the evening a meeting was held at First Avenue and Fayette Street. There was a large audience of men and women and Burgess Bloomhall introduced Mrs. Gertrude Fuller of Pittsburgh as the speaker. She held her audience in rapt attention, and was often cheered.

Mrs. Fuller made an admirable address and a strong argument in favor of equal suffrage. The women who want to vote, she said, are the women who work for a living. They want to vote for a law that will give them a minimum wage, give better sanitation, better protection against machinery, and better living conditions. She claimed that women who do the same work as men receive fifty percent of the wages paid to men, but if they had the franchise, the manufacturers would be compelled by law to pay the same wages. Equal suffrage means equal wages. That is why the working women want to vote.

Mrs. Fuller witnessed a number of strikes at close range and she said that women strike because they cannot get their grievances redressed any other way. If they could vote, they would not strike, because their demands would result in the enactment of laws that would give them equal wages with men, and correct the many other inequalities that they must suffer.

The campaign party remained here overnight and left town this morning in a gaily decorated automobile escorting the bell to Philadelphia where it will be in a prominent place in the procession of the Festival of Light to be held tonight.
Conshohocken (PA) Recorder, October 22, 1915

Suffragists Greet Liberty Bell on Its Way into the City: Mainline Suburbs a Blaze of Yellow as the Precious Symbol Passes Through Them Decorated for Parade

Blazes of yellow, the suffrage color, greeted the woman's Liberty Bell along the Main Line today as the replica of the nation's Liberty Bell slowly and in triumph, but with its clapper symbolically tied, was brought to the city where it will take part tonight in the Festival of Light, the first night parade ever held by Philadelphia suffragists.

The bell and its auto truck, surrounded by a fleet of convoying automobiles, received an ovation from Conshohocken to Overbrook as it returned from its Statewide tour. Starting at Conshohocken at 9:30 am in the charge of Miss Helen Clark, secretary of the Pennsylvania Woman Suffrage Association, stops were made at Villanova, Rosemont, Bryn Mawr, Haverford, Haverford College, and Ardmore, the caravan gathering in strength as the city was neared.

A huge laurel wreath was placed on the truck at Ardmore by Mrs. James D. Winsor [Rebecca Chapman Winsor], Lower Merion suffrage leader. Among those who accompanied the bell in automobiles were Mrs. M. J. Ensign [Mary Jenkins Ensign], Mrs. J. Howard Brown, Mrs. Clement A. Griscom, Mrs. Edward Y. Hartshorne, Mrs. Ferree Brinton and Dr. Bertha Lewis.

A large delegation of Philadelphia suffragists officially welcomed the bell at Overbrook, where it was shrouded. It was then brought to the city to be turned over to the corps of electricians for decoration with lights.

Bell Being Decorated

The parade will be a picturesque and spectacular culmination of an unprecedented campaign of activity on the part of Pennsylvania suffragists to convince the electorate of the state of the need and justice of woman's enfranchisement.

Starting at Broad and Mifflin Streets, thousands of women, on foot, and in motor, together with hundreds of men sympathizers, will comprise a torchlight procession that for sheer beauty and artistic effect is expected to rival any pageant ever held before.

With its clapper tied to symbolize the voiceless condition of women, and accompanied by its escort of State suffrage officers and the suffrage pioneers, Mrs. Charlotte Pierce, Mrs. Jane Campbell, and Miss Anna Hancock, the bell will head the procession, its truck drawn by a cohort of 50 young suffragists.

Searchlights, Greek fire and a colorful mass of lanterns will furnish the illumination. Virtually all of the Philadelphia organizations and those of neighboring counties will be represented. Visiting leagues from nearby states have also been assigned the places in line. It has been estimated that twice the number of enthusiasts who made the demonstration of May such a notable affair will march tonight, and three or four times the number of citizens who lined the sidewalks and took their places in windows and on roofs to watch them are expected to come forth tonight because of the fact that the parade is being held after office hours.

A busy bee atmosphere has characterized the headquarters of local organizations for the last month. Costumes have been planned and floats and transparencies designed. Tonight will show the result.

Evening Public Ledger (Philadelphia, PA), October 22, 1915

SUFFRAGIST SPOTLIGHT

Mary Jenkins Ensign (1857–1936)

Mary Jenkins Ensign, 1902.

Mary Jenkins Kamas was born on December 12, 1857, the youngest of three children of Joshua Kamas and Sarah Elizabeth Jenkins Kamas. She married Henry LeGrand Ensign, a lawyer, around 1884. The couple had no children. By 1890, they were living in Ardmore, Pennsylvania, a suburb of Philadelphia, and were both active in the community.

In 1897, Mary Jenkins Ensign became editor of the *Ardmore Chronicle*, a local newspaper, and by 1906 she was listed as its publisher. In 1911, she was appointed postmaster of Ardmore, a position she held until 1914.[68] In 1915, she chaired the Woman's Suffrage Press and Publicity Committee for Montgomery County.

As editor and publisher of the *Ardmore Chronicle*, she published numerous articles on women's issues, including suffrage, the temperance movement, and violence against women. To print the newspaper, she used the woman-run Ardmore Printing Company.[69]

On May 1, 1915, Ensign issued a sixteen-page special edition on women's suffrage, which she mailed to every voter in her district. In her "Letter from the Editor and Publisher," she wrote:

> Under the caption, 'Women Ask Fair Play of Men,' we publish today a Special Suffrage Issue of "The Chronicle." The believers in Equal Suffrage for Women have long since realized that newspapers are the best distributors of news and have not been slow to use them as a means of spreading broadcast the message of Equal Suffrage.
>
> On our part, we have given hearty cooperation, because we believe that Equal Suffrage will be most beneficial to both men and women, and best for the good of all.
>
> "The Chronicle" has ever stood and will continue to stand for all the best in our community, our Township, our County, our State and our Nation. Progress has been our watchword since the publication of the first sheet, and today we feel that in presenting this message of Equal Suffrage for Women that we are taking another step forward and keeping pace with the spirit of the age in which we live.[70]

The Justice Bell party traveled through Ardmore on October 22, 1915, where Ensign was photographed placing a wreath on the bell.[71] She also made several speeches from the bell truck.

It is unclear when Mary Jenkins Ensign and her husband divorced, but by 1924 she was living with Lillian Burr. The 1930 census lists Burr as Ensign's partner. When Ensign died on February 18, 1936, at the age of seventy-eight, she left her estate and belongings to Burr, who served as her executor.

Woman Suffrage Parade

PHILADELPHIA

On Friday Evening, October 22nd, 1915

Thousands of earnest Men and Women marching in a

GRAND FESTIVAL OF LIGHT

Forming on South Broad Street, at Mifflin, march up Broad Street, around City Hall, to

ACADEMY OF MUSIC

where a great Mass Meeting will be held.

Men and Women, get into line, four abreast, at 6.45 o'clock sharp,

RAIN OR SHINE

March for your convictions

March for justice to women

Bring your friends, men and women

Women wear white (not essential)

Watch your step—keep in step with the music

Carry torch or lantern (if possible)

Carry an American Flag (if you have one)

WOMAN'S JUSTICE BELL

(Silent until Women have the Vote)

1776
Liberty
Independence

1915
Justice
Equality

A duplicate of the old Liberty Bell, which is to ring for the first time on the day that the women of Pennsylvania are granted the right to vote.

The Liberty Bell of 1776 rang to proclaim Liberty and Independence—to create a nation; the Woman's Justice Bell will ring to establish Justice and Equality—to complete and perfect a nation.

Let every just man help break the chain that holds the clapper silent.

THE WOMAN'S JUSTICE BELL

soon to become famous, will be in the great Parade.

SHOW YOUR COLORS. MARCH WITH US ON OCTOBER 22ND

GIVE THE WOMEN A SQUARE DEAL BY VOTING "YES" ON NOVEMBER 2ND

Send word that you will march, to ANNA H. SNYDER, Secretary Parade Committee, 1723 Chestnut Street, or to any Suffrage Headquarters.

Flyer for the Festival of Light parade held in Philadelphia, October 22, 1915.

PHILADELPHIA COUNTY (October 22–24)

8,000 March in Philadelphia: Suffrage Parade to Welcome the Women's Justice Bell: Special to the New York Times

Philadelphia, Pa., Oct. 22—This was woman suffrage night in Philadelphia. Eight thousand men and women advocates of the cause, bearing torches and lanterns and bedecked in a hundred varieties of uniforms, marched on Broad Street in what was called a Festival of Light. One hundred thousand persons witnessed the spectacle, which culminated in a mass meeting in the Academy of Music. Five thousand persons who could not gain admittance to the hall formed the audience in an overflow meeting outside. The occasion was the arrival after its long tour of the Woman's Justice Bell. Resting on a bank of flowers, completely hiding the wheels upon which it rolled, the bell was drawn over the streets by 100 young women dressed in white, flowing garments, garlanded with daffodils. The "Yellow Suffrage" automobile of Dr. Anna Howard Shaw also appeared in the procession.

Women representing every profession, trade union, college, and of course, suffrage organizations, as well as men from every line of endeavor were in line, and only the aged rode. Many costumes were striking and novel.

Speakers in the Academy of Music included Norman Hapgood, George Creel, Commissioner Katharine Bement Davis of New York, Senator Moses E. Clapp of Minnesota, and Jennie Bradley Roessing.

New York Times, October 23, 1915

DELAWARE COUNTY (October 25–27)

Bell's Welcome into the County: Enthusiastic Greetings All Along the Chester and Darby Pikes to the City

Yesterday marked another distinct epoch in the history of the famous Woman's Liberty Bell, which has been transported on its tour through the state. Handed over to the Delaware County suffrage officials by the officials from the City of Brotherly Love, in front of the historic Blue Bell Inn, near the dividing line between Philadelphia and Delaware County, the replica of the sacred Liberty Bell traversed much of the same historic ground in its triumphal march through Delaware County that was covered by Washington and his gallant Continental Army after the Battle of the Brandywine.

At the old Blue Bell, the suffrage bell was handed over by the Philadelphia chairman to Mrs. J. Claude Bedford of Media, Delaware County chairman.

Delaware County Times (Chester, PA), October 26, 1915

Bell's Tour in the County: Boroughs and Towns Give Emblem of Liberty an Enthusiastic Reception

The Liberty Bell of Woman's Suffrage concluded its journey through this county yesterday, accompanied by women in automobiles, and as the bell wended its way through the different boroughs and hamlets in the eastern section of the county, speeches were made in the interest of Suffrage. At each of the places, demonstrations were held. The bell was turned over to the Woman Suffrage Party of Chester County, its first entrance into that county being at Berwyn.

Everywhere the bell went accompanied by Woman's Suffrage workers, it was received by enthusiastic crowds, and the men in particular were very courteous to the speakers. The trip was in charge of Mrs. Claude Bedford, of Media, Chairman of the Delaware County Suffrage Party.

The bell left Media at 10 o'clock for Swarthmore, and after a demonstration in that borough, Miss Helen Todd, of California, and Mrs. J. Claude Bedford made speeches. The next stop was in Clifton Heights. At this place the party began to increase in numbers, more automobiles taking up the rear of the procession. The bell was brought to a halt in front of the First National Bank of Clifton Heights, and here it was greeted by a large audience made up of men who were going home from the factories for their noon day lunch, children of the public schools, and many other men and women, and the Clifton Heights branch of the Woman's Suffrage Party.

Mrs. J. Claude Bedford opened the meeting and made an address which was short but forceful. Miss Todd was then introduced, and gave an interesting history of the success of

Woman's Suffrage in her own state. Miss Todd said that women should have as much right to vote as men, and that if given the opportunity to vote, will do so in such a way that it will bring brighter days for the people of this state. Miss Todd is a convincing talker and her address was listened to with much interest.

From Clifton Heights, the bell procession started for Aldan ... after which the bell proceeded to Lansdowne. At this place the bell was given a great ovation. N. Barton Masters, pastor of the Lansdowne Methodist Church, made the opening speech. Miss Todd, Mrs. Bedford, and Mrs. Anne Wallace Ladomus made speeches. The bell, after the demonstration, proceeded to Llanerch, to Oakmont, Preston, Garrett Hill, all in Radnor township. At 7 o'clock there was a big demonstration in Wayne where addresses were made by Miss Todd, Mrs. Bedford, and others. After the demonstration, the bell journeyed to Berwyn, Chester County, where it starts on another journey. Mrs. Bedford was highly pleased with the reception the bell and speakers received.

Delaware County Times (Chester, PA), October 28, 1915

Alice Bedford (1877–1960)

Alice Bedford, 1918.

Alice Bedford was born Alice Katharine Huey in Philadelphia on June 27, 1877, the daughter of Robert Huey, a dentist, and Katharine Cowpland Goepp (or Goepf). On May 5, 1902, she married John Claude Bedford, a professor of law at Temple University, who had been elected the previous year as a Fusion Democrat to the Pennsylvania House of Representatives, where he served one term. The couple had four daughters.[72]

In 1912, Bedford served as a delegate representing Delaware County at the National Woman Suffrage Convention in Philadelphia.[73] The following year, she was elected chair of the Woman Suffrage Party of Delaware County, a position she held until December 1915.[74] She was instrumental in building a strong county organization and sponsored numerous events that contributed to the 1915 Votes for Women campaign.

As chair of the Woman's Suffrage Party of Delaware County, Bedford hosted Alice Dunbar at two events on September 18, 1915, one at the Media Armory and the other in Chadds Ford.[75]

On October 25, 1915, Bedford led the Delaware County suffrage delegation that received the Justice Bell from the Philadelphia delegation at the historic Blue Bell Inn. Accompanying her were Mrs. A. B. Geary, second vice county chairman; Miss Ruth Verlenden of Darby, leader of the second legislative district; and a large number of suffrage workers. Two meetings were held, one inside and one outside, for the employees of Fels Soap Works, whose factory stood opposite the Blue Bell Inn.[76] During the bell's time in Delaware County, Bedford delivered speeches from the bell truck, including in Clifton Heights, Lansdowne, and Wayne.[77]

After women won the vote, Bedford continued her advocacy for social causes and civic improvement. She held several leadership roles, including as the first president of the Republican Women's Club of Delaware County and as founder and first president of the Delaware County Women's Committee of the Philadelphia Orchestra.

Alice Bedford died on October 15, 1960, at the age of eighty-three.[78]

CHESTER COUNTY (October 28–30)

> ***Suffrage Bell Ends Long Tour: West Chester People Give It a Noble Welcome to Town***
>
> Making a tour of 5,000 miles, the Woman's Suffrage Bell, having visited every county in the State, halted in front of the Court House Saturday evening a little after 5 o'clock. With it was tremendous crowds which filled the portico and steps, the lawn and the neighboring street. One of the largest and most attentive audiences in the history of the town stood to look and listen while speaker after speaker told the story of the campaign and predicted that women one day will vote side-by-side with their husbands and brethren.

> As the big motor truck which carries the bell was backed in against the curb in a space cleared for it by Officer Edgar Jackson, Mrs. Katharine W. Ruschenberger, donor of the bell, said to a friend:
>
> "It is here that we rest our case. The bell comes back to its own home after making a complete tour of the state and standing in front of Independence Hall, Philadelphia, only a few yards from the Liberty Bell, of which it is counterpart. It has been a great success, a leading feature in the campaign.
>
> "This is the home of the bell because in June 1852, the first woman's suffrage meeting in Pennsylvania was held in West Chester, with James and Lucretia Mott and many other speakers present.
>
> "We have made our plea over the state, and now our case rests upon these two principles which are the basic principles upon which the United States is founded, 'No taxation without representation,' and 'All governments derive their just powers from the consent of the governed.'"
>
> By this time the crowd had settled down to an orderly meeting, and the regular speaking began.
>
> *Daily Local News* (West Chester, PA), November 1, 1915

After their long journey, the exhausted but jubilant suffragists would now wait for the November 2 election results. They were confident that the men would vote "yes" on Amendment One, finally granting the state's women the right to vote.

As reported on November 1, 1915, Jennie Bradley Roessing expressed her faith in the male voters: "Men of Pennsylvania, your wives, mothers, sisters and daughters ask you to give our state justice to its women . . . . We believe that when you go to the polls tomorrow you will remember that the sole impulse behind our request for the ballot is the desire to help produce a better and equitable civilization. We believe in your sense of fair play, and in this spirit of faith and comradeship, we rest our case in your hands."[79]

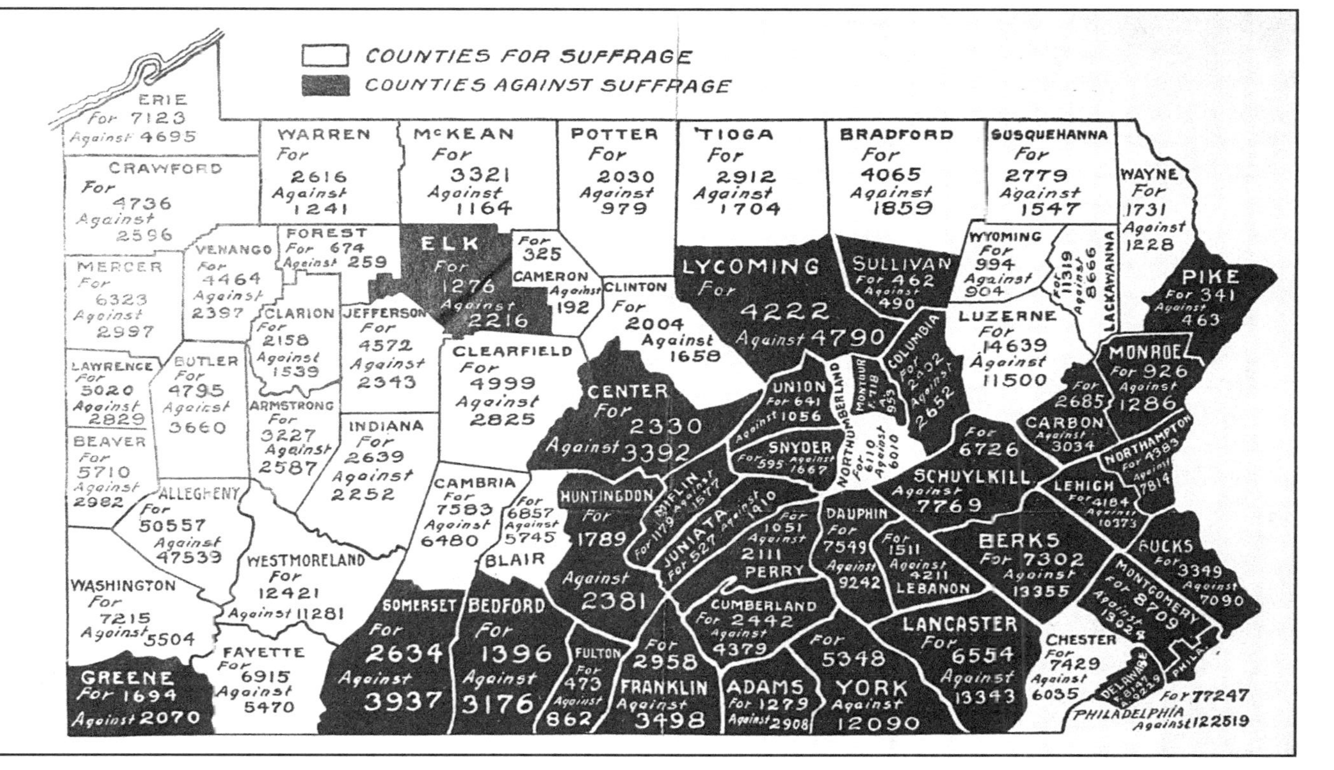

A 1915 map depicting vote totals by county for or against women's suffrage n Pennsylvania.

Election Day
November 2, 1915

As election results trickled in on November 3, the suffragists read the newspaper headlines with shock and disbelief: the suffrage amendment had failed. Initial numbers showed that, of the 826,382 votes cast, Amendment One lost by 100,000 votes—a figure later adjusted to 55,686 votes, of which 45,272 came from Philadelphia. Of the sixty-seven counties, thirty-three voted "yes" for women's suffrage. In general, the men of the western and northern counties voted in the affirmative, while the eastern and southern counties largely voted against the amendment, with the most significant defeat coming from Philadelphia.

Farming and rural communities overall supported the amendment. Two of the largest anthracite coal counties, Lackawanna and Luzerne, including the towns of Scranton and Wilkes-Barre, voted for the amendment, undoubtedly due to the work of powerhouse Kate Chapman, chair of the Lackawanna County chapter of the PWSA. Chapman oversaw not only of Lackawanna but also the surrounding counties.

Berks, Lebanon, and Lehigh Counties' losses were reported as due largely to Pennsylvania Germans, who voted overwhelmingly against the amendment. In Schuylkill County, where an adverse vote of 10,000–15,000 was predicted, the amendment lost by only 1,043 votes. Credit was given to Helen Beddall of Pottsville, chair of the Schuylkill County suffrage organization, who conducted a persistent campaign of education for two years prior to the election.

Liquor companies had worked nonstop to block the amendment and were successful in many counties. Although a powerful force in Erie County, their efforts there were unsuccessful, no doubt in part because of the efforts of Augusta Fleming, who had worked to keep prohibition reforms out of women's suffrage speeches.

Ruschenberger's home county, Chester County, was the only one of the southeastern counties in which a majority of men voted for women's suffrage. On behalf of Ruschenberger and the women of the Woman's Suffrage Party of Chester County, their chair sent out an official thank you to the local papers:[80]

> The Woman's Suffrage Party of Chester County desires to thank the men of Chester County for the uniform kindness shown women at the polls, and for placing themselves on record

by such a large majority as in favor of justice and fair play.

The first suffrage meeting was held in Chester County in 1852. The share taken by her men and women in aiding the slave to achieve freedom and justice is well known. It is fitting, therefore, that in this second struggle for justice, Chester County should again lead the earlier counties, and her men emphatically register their belief in trusting the women, whom they so unhesitatingly trust with the deepest interests of their daily lives, with greater power to help them in their mutual struggle for the common good.

We thank you for this vindication of our faith in the truth of our slogan:

"Chester County women believe in Chester County men; Chester County men believe in Chester County women."

We shall try to justify your faith by our works.

Gertrude Grouveneur Smith, Chairman Woman's Suffrage Party of Chester County[81]

Because of Pennsylvania's five-year rule for introducing amendments, the movement would have to wait until 1920 to once again get a suffrage amendment on the ballot. Many women abandoned the state effort and turned their attention to fighting for a federal amendment.[82]

PART THREE

After the Tour

Four unidentified women with the Justice Bell in Washington, DC, December 1915.

1915: The Justice Bell Travels to Washington, DC

A month after the defeat of the women's suffrage amendments in Pennsylvania, New York, Massachusetts, and New Jersey, Louise Hall and Elizabeth McShane accompanied the Justice Bell to Washington, DC, at the direction of Katharine Ruschenberger. They joined suffragists from across the country for a December 7 parade advocating for a federal amendment to the Constitution. The march was planned to coincide with the start of the 64th Congress and the first convention of the Congressional Union for Woman Suffrage, an organization led by Alice Paul.

The main event was to welcome the western envoys, Sara Bard Field and Frances Jolliffe, who had driven across the country from San Francisco with a petition for President Wilson that was filled with signatures from women in the western states demanding a federal amendment granting women the right to vote. Swedish suffragists were in charge of the car, with Maria Kindberg driving and Ingeborg Kindstedt serving as the mechanic during the arduous journey. The *Washington Post* reported on the event:

> ***President Hears Suffrage Plea After Congress Gets Big Petition: Big Bell Feature of the Parade***
>
> Mrs. John J. White, grand marshal, accompanied by a mounted escort of women dressed in flowing robes of purple, white, and yellow, the suffrage colors, formed a body guard for the envoys. Twelve girl colorbearers preceded the main body of the parade, which was made up of 300 women on foot and horseback.
>
> A feature of the parade was the woman's liberty bell, which was carried through Pennsylvania during the recent campaign there. The bell, which is about three feet in diameter, was mounted on a large truck.
>
> Thousands of suffrage banners were carried in the parade and flung to the breezes from the windows and housetops along the line of the march. A huge Susan B. Anthony banner bearing the words "We Demand the Passage of the Bristol-Mondell Amendment" [the Susan B. Anthony Amendment] was carried near the head of the pageant by four women.
>
> The biting wind all but tore the banners and pennants from the marchers' hands.

> After receiving assurance from both houses of Congress that suffrage would be considered at an early meeting of that body, the suffragists again formed in line and proceeded up Pennsylvania avenue to the White House.
> *Washington Post* (Washington, DC), December 7, 1915

After the trip to Washington, Ruschenberger moved the Justice Bell to a garage in Chester County.

1916: The Justice Bell Travels to Chicago

The 1916 Republican National Convention was scheduled to be held in Chicago from June 7 to 10. The suffragists wanted the Republicans to include a women's suffrage plank in their platform and seized the opportunity to convince them by holding their own events in Chicago at the same time.[1] The Congressional Union for Woman Suffrage, later renamed the National Woman's Party (NWP), held its first convention, and the National American Woman Suffrage Association (NAWSA) scheduled a national drive for suffrage to begin in Chicago with a large suffrage parade. A delegation of Pennsylvania suffragists that included Katharine Ruschenberger traveled by train to Chicago, where the Justice Bell had already been taken to be a central feature of the parade, which took place on June 7 during a torrential downpour. After hours of debate, the Republicans finally accepted a women's suffrage plank.[2]

On June 15, 1916, Washington's *Daily Herald* interviewed Mary Orlady (Mrs. George B. Orlady), who had been voted president of the PWSA the previous December:

> "We went to Chicago hopeful that the Republican principles recognize the political equality as well as social equality of women.
>
> By inserting the woman suffrage plank in their platform, the Republican party at last has proved, as it has often said, that ours is a government of the people, by the people and for the people. By its plank, the Republican party has said further that it believes that women, as we have ever contended, should have a voice in the government that governs them; have a voice in the making of the laws that they as well as men must obey . . . .
>
> Despite the down pouring rain and the pressing atmospheric

> conditions, not a single woman in the Pennsylvania delegation of suffragists flinched, but marched down Michigan Avenue in our big suffrage parade. Most impressive among the many impressive features, was our Woman's Liberty Bell, the silent symbol of suffrage originated by Mrs. Charles Ruschenberger of Strafford, Pennsylvania, and sent to Chicago by the Pennsylvania Men's League for Woman Suffrage, of which Mr. Wilmer Atkinson of Philadelphia is president.
>
> Decorated with American flags and a large sign to the effect that it, the replica of the Liberty Bell, would not sound until the women of Pennsylvania were given the vote, [the bell has] attracted the interest and attention of thousands."[3]

During the same month, the Democratic National Convention held their convention in St. Louis, Missouri, from June 14 to June 16. To convince the men of the party to include a women's suffrage plank in its platform, suffragists created a "walkless talkless parade" on the first day of the convention. Lining the route the delegates had to walk from their hotel to the convention hall, the suffragists wore golden sashes and held yellow parasols and signs with the words "Votes for Women." They called it the Golden Lane. Their effort was successful.

1917: The Justice Bell Is Stored in a Garage

During 1917, while many Pennsylvania women were in Washington, DC, picketing in front of the White House, the Justice Bell was stored in a garage in Strafford, the hometown of Katharine Ruschenberger. The bell had been requested to help stimulate interest in Liberty Bond sales, but Ruschenberger turned the organizers down, saying the bell was purely a suffrage bell.

Ruschenberger supported the National Woman's Party's campaign for the federal amendment, and in August 1917, she told a reporter of West Chester's *Daily Local News*, "It is to ring for the completion of democracy in the United States of America, and the enfranchisement of all Americans. The bell believes in the passing of a federal amendment, and in this cause, may go to Washington."[4] There is no evidence that the Justice Bell went to Washington, DC, in 1917. It did, however, despite apparent Ruschenberger's objection, travel there in 1918 to appear in a Liberty Loan parade.

1918: The Justice Bell is Highlighted and Repurposed

In March, 1918, Ruschenberger traveled to Washington, DC with a letter and a framed photograph of the Justice Bell for every US senator. As reported in the *Washington Herald* on March 4, 1918:

> Beside the desk of every Senator in Washington, the suffragists of Pennsylvania have hung a picture of the "Woman's Liberty Bell," chained and waiting to ring when the women of the country shall have been granted the vote.
>
> A photograph of the bell has been presented to each senator by Mrs. Charles Wister Ruschenberger and Miss Ella Rigel, both of Philadelphia, who acted as representatives of the Justice Bell Committee of Pennsylvania.
>
> *Is Bronze Replica*
>
> The "Woman's Liberty Bell" is a bronze replica of the Liberty Bell of 1776 and belongs to Pennsylvania suffragists. It is also known as the "Justice Bell." During the last suffrage campaign, the bell toured the state from one end to the other. It was originated by Mrs. Ruschenberger, who conceived that the original Liberty Bell had cracked because it had not been able to endure the fact that only half of the people of the country had liberty.
>
> The letter presented to the senators with the picture of the bell is as follows:
>
> "My dear Senator: With this letter is sent you a framed photograph, which we hope you will find worthy to hang at your desk.
>
> "The Justice Bell is a replica in bronze, exact weight and size of the Liberty Bell of 1776. Cast March 31, 1915, after a meeting of suffragists held in Independence Hall, Philadelphia, PA, for purpose as follows: Upon the enfranchisement of women, an act of national justice, to ring to 'establish justice' to be America's second great national ideal. Men gave liberty. Women would establish justice. And upon the enfranchisement of women to 'proclaim' the fulfillment of liberty and the completion of democracy in the United States of America.
>
> *"Would Add 'Justice'"*
>
> "The French nation upon the grave of the first Americans to fall in France has placed these words, "Here rest the soldiers

> of the illustrious republic of the United States who fell in France for Justice and Liberty.
>
> "Will you not help us to unchain the Justice Bell by voting for the Federal suffrage amendment for woman suffrage in the Senate, that our bell may ring and the world may know that to 'Liberty' America has added 'Justice.'"
>
> (Signed) K. W. Ruschenberger, Chairman and National Custodian[5]

Although there is no record of Ruschenberger participating, the Justice Bell did appear as a Liberty Bell replica, in the Third Liberty Loan parade in Washington, DC, on April 26, 1918.[6] The bell seemed to be partly under the supervision of Antoinette Funk, who had been a Justice Bell tour speaker in 1915 and was now vice chair of the Woman's National Liberty Loan Committee. Funk participated in that parade as part of the women's division. There was only a brief mention in the newspapers of the bell's suffrage origins.[7]

On September 28, 1918, the Justice Bell, temporarily rechristened the Victory Bell, rode on a float in front of the women's division in the Philadelphia parade as part of the Fourth Liberty Loan Drive. At the time, it was the largest parade ever held in Philadelphia. Later the parade became infamous for spreading the Spanish Flu, which resulted in thousands of deaths.[8]

1919: The Justice Bell Travels to Harrisburg

On June 4, 1919, more than a year after Ruschenberger's appeal to the senators, Congress finally passed the Nineteenth Amendment, a federal amendment that would grant women across the nation the right to vote. It stated: "The right of citizens of the United States to vote shall not be denied or abridged by the United States or by any State on account of sex. Congress shall have power to enforce this article by appropriate legislation."

Thirty-six state legislatures would have to ratify it by a majority vote in order for it to be added to the United States Constitution. The first to vote for ratification were the state legislatures of Wisconsin, Illinois, and Michigan on June 10, 1919.

On June 19, 1919, the Pennsylvania State Senate adopted the resolution to ratify the Nineteenth Amendment. In anticipation of the upcoming House vote, the Justice Bell was brought to Harrisburg for a suffrage parade, and women from every part of the state gathered at the state capitol.

On June 24, 1919, the Pennsylvania House of Representatives cast its vote. With a final tally of 153 in favor and 44 against, Pennsylvania became the seventh state to ratify the Nineteenth Amendment.[9] Yellow balloons were released by many of the representatives and batted around the chamber as the women cheered from the gallery.

Rep. Robert Lauder Wallace of Lawrence County requested a two-minute recess so that Lucy Kennedy Miller could thank the men. For this purpose, and for the first time in the history of the Pennsylvania legislature, a woman was permitted to address the House of Representatives from the Speaker's chair. The *Pittsburgh Post-Gazette* reported her speech:

> We appreciate the honor accorded the Pennsylvania Suffrage Association and allowing me, its president, to extend the sincere thanks of the organization to the legislature. You have today done the biggest thing you have ever done in your history . . . . We want to thank all of our old and new friends, the speaker, the leaders of the Senate, Mr. [William T.] Ramsey [Delaware County representative], and especially the governor. To him, we owe the deepest debt of gratitude. We thank the reporters, whether they have been for or against us, for they have been fair in the treatment of our cause. I do not believe any men in the House will regret his action today in assisting the women to come into the voting ranks in 1920.[10]

Over the following months, more states approved the amendment, with Washington becoming the thirty-fifth state to ratify it on March 22, 1920. It took another five months before Tennessee finally ratified it on August 18, 1920, becoming the thirty-sixth and final state needed for the Nineteenth Amendment to be added to the US Constitution.

The vote in the Tennessee legislature passed by only one vote, cast by twenty-four-year-old Harry Burn who had initially planned to vote "no." In the end, he supported the amendment because his mother, Phoebe "Febb" Burn, urged him to. Newspapers reported his reasoning: "I know that a mother's advice is always safest for her boy to follow, and my mother wanted me to vote for the ratification."[11]

The Nineteenth Amendment was officially certified on August 26, 1920, a date now celebrated annually as Women's Equality Day. Although additional state approvals were not required for ratification, votes from the remaining states trickled in over the following decades, with Mississippi becoming the final state to ratify the amendment in 1984.

The League of Women Voters

In anticipation of women gaining the right to vote, the National American Woman Suffrage Association reorganized as the League of Women Voters on February 14, 1920. Its mission was to encourage women to take full advantage of their newfound power, including guidance on the mechanics of voting—how to register, how ballots worked, and what to expect at the polls. Suffragists who had spent years in the trenches of the fight were eager to help their sisters prepare for their first election. With only a few months to get ready, they would help choose a new president on November 2. Warren G. Harding and his running mate, Calvin Coolidge, won in a landslide.

On September 21, 1920, Philadelphia's *Evening Public Ledger* reported a letter sent to Mayor J. Hampton Moore from the Philadelphia League of Women Voters:

> The Philadelphia League of Women Voters and joint committee of organizations accept for themselves and for the women voters of Pennsylvania and as a nation the invitation of Mayor Moore for a national reception to be held at Independence Square on Saturday, September 25, at 3 p.m. In honor of this occasion, and to mark the new era into which the nation is entering, we will ring for the first time our Justice Bell, a bronze replica of the Liberty Bell, cast on March 31, 1915, to proclaim completion of democracy in the United States of America, and to establish justice. Men gave liberty to America and to the world. Women will bring to the nation as their gift, justice.[12]

Mayor Moore, who was not a supporter of women's suffrage, gave the celebrants strict instructions, as reported in the *Evening Public Ledger*: "At the suggestion of Mayor Moore, who will preside, the exercises will be simple as the women can make them. There will be no flaunting of suffrage banners. Instead of the suffrage yellow, the predominant color scheme will be the patriotic colors, red, white, and blue. The city's chief executive deems this color fashion more suitable to the historic environment of the birthplace of American freedom."[13]

Katharine Wentworth, Katharine Ruschenberger's niece, rehearses ringing the Justice Bell in Independence Square, September 24, 1920.

1920: The Justice Bell Rings

On September 25, 1920, Pennsylvania celebrated. The *Evening Public Ledger* headline announced, "Justice Bell to Peal Tidings of Woman's Victory," and the article stated: "The women of Philadelphia will proclaim the political emancipation of themselves and their American sisters at a great victory jubilation in Independence Square this afternoon. Just as their great-great grandfathers had in 1776 rang out joyful tidings of their independence of Great Britain, the American sisterhood today will toll the "Woman's Justice Bell" proclaiming "liberty throughout all the land unto all the inhabitants thereof."[14]

Katharine Ruschenberger took her seat on the platform and watched as thousands of people filled Philadelphia's Independence Square. Her role was to speak about the featured guest of honor, the Justice Bell.

After community singing and a concert by the police band, Mayor J. Hampton Moore opened the day's events with a speech, followed by an invocation by Rev. Frederick R. Griffin of the First Unitarian Church of Philadelphia. Governor William C. Sproul of Pennsylvania spoke, declaring, "To my opinion, this is one of the four greatest occasions in American history. The first was the Declaration of Independence; the second, the adoption of our Constitution; the third, the wiping out of slavery; and fourth, the accomplishment of equal rights for women."[15]

Other speakers included Florence Lukens Piersol (Mrs. George A. Piersol), chair of the Philadelphia League of Women Voters; Lucy Kennedy Miller, chair of the League of Women Voters of Pennsylvania; Maud Wood Park, national president of the League of Women Voters; and Dr. M. Carey Thomas, president of Bryn Mawr College.

Attendees included two nieces of Susan B. Anthony, Ann Anthony Bacon and Lucy E. Anthony. The latter wore a diamond-studded pin in the shape of a flag, which had been presented to her aunt by the women of Wyoming in 1900 to commemorate the first granting of the vote to women in 1869.[16]

As Ruschenberger observed the event, she must have reflected on how long it had taken to reach this day:

Seventy-two years had passed since the 1848 Seneca Falls Convention, led by Lucretia Mott, Elizabeth Cady Stanton, Mary Ann M'Clintock, Martha Coffin Wright, and Jane Hunt.

Forty-eight years had passed since Susan B. Anthony registered and voted in New York—an act for which she was promptly arrested, put on trial, and fined.

Thirty years had passed since the American Woman Suffrage Association and the National Woman Suffrage Association united to form the National American Woman Suffrage Association (NAWSA).

Seven years earlier, on March 3, 1913, the day before President Woodrow Wilson's inauguration, a suffrage parade of ten thousand people, organized by Alice Paul and led by Inez Milholland riding on a white horse, marched down Pennsylvania Avenue in Washington, DC. The parade diverted the nation's attention from the inauguration due to its size, pageantry, and the scandal of mobs attacking the women while the police turned away.

Only three years before the Nineteenth Amendment was ratified, Alice Paul and others began picketing in front of the White House. Known as the Silent Sentinels, many of the women, including Justice Bell tour director Elizabeth McShane, suffered terrible abuse. During that period, more than five hundred women were arrested, and many endured assaults, beatings, and even further cruelty while on hunger strikes protesting their incarceration.

Finally, two years before ratification, on January 10, 1918, the United States House of Representatives voted in favor of the suffrage amendment. The Senate did not pass it until June 4, 1919—using the same wording that Susan B. Anthony had written in 1878 and that had been reintroduced to each session of every Congress over the following four decades: "The right of citizens of the United States to vote shall not be denied or abridged by the United States or by any State on account of sex. Congress shall have power to enforce this article by appropriate legislation."

After Tennessee ratified the amendment on August 18, 1920, the Nineteenth Amendment was officially added to the Constitution on August 26, 1920.

Carrie Chapman Catt, president of the National American Woman Suffrage Association, described the long struggle: "To get the word 'male' in effect out of the Constitution, cost the women of the country fifty-two years of pauseless campaign . . . . During that time, they were forced to conduct 56 campaigns of referenda to male voters; 480 campaigns to get legislatures to submit suffrage amendments to voters; 47 campaigns to get State constitutional conventions to write woman suffrage into state constitutions; 277 campaigns to get State party conventions to include woman suffrage planks in party platforms; and 19 campaigns with 19 successive Congresses."[17]

No one could deny that women's right to vote had been hard-won over many years and through the efforts of hundreds of thousands of women.

Now, Ruschenberger stood on a stage as her beloved Justice Bell took a place of honor on the day the clapper would be freed to ring the bell for the first time. As she stepped forward to begin her speech, she beckoned her brother's daughter, Katharine Wentworth, to prepare to ring the bell. This was the same niece who had joined her aunt during the March 31, 1915, event celebrating the casting of the Justice Bell at the Meneely Bell Company in Troy, New York.

As Ruschenberger began her speech recounting the history and significance of the Justice Bell, women representatives from every state began their procession to the stage. Katharine Wentworth rang the bell three times before others took over, ringing it forty-five more times—once for each state. Across the country, women and men rang their own bells in celebratory solidarity.

PART FOUR

What Happened to the Justice Bell?

TO HOUSE "JUSTICE BELL"

Suffrage Leaders Plan Tower for Independence Square

Women suffrage leaders of Philadelphia and vicinity are planning to construct a tower to house the "Justice Bell," which now reposes temporarily, without special setting, in League Island Park.

Several prominent architects have offered to design the tower, according to Mrs. Charles Wister Ruschenberger, of Stafford. Construction cost would be borne by suffragists' contributions. Mrs. Ruschenberger and her associates hope to obtain permission from the municipal authorities to erect the proposed tower in Independence Square.

Suffragists make plan to house Justice Bell in a "Citizenship Tower," March 3, 1921.

BIG SUFFRAGE BELL FALLEN FROM GRACE

Woman's Symbol of Right to Vote Rests in City Slaughter House

Workmen Threaten to Throw Relic on Dump If It Is Not Removed

Report of the Justice Bell's relocation to a Philadelphia slaughterhouse, May 26, 1921.

'Justice' Bell Seeks a Shrine

Twenty years ago they marched, shouted and sang in the cause of women's suffrage.

Finally they won the 19th Amendment to the Constitution, giving women the voting franchise, and marked their triumph by pealing out their "Justice" bell in Independence Hall.

And yesterday, in connection with the 150th anniversary of the ratification of the Constitution, women were called upon to provide a proper setting for the "Justice" bell, which hangs now in the Washington Memorial Chapel at Valley Forge.

Mrs. Catharine Wentworth Ruschenberger, of Strafford, who led the drive to buy the "Justice" bell—a one-ton bronze replica of the Liberty Bell—declared it "belongs to all women" and that it deserved an adequate care of its own.

"The bell signifies justice," the white-haired leader said, "and justice is the most important thing in the world today. We have won our liberty; now we must fight to preserve justice. The Nation should recognize the importance of this bell, and help its maintenance."

Ruschenberger searches for a new home for the Justice Bell, June 23, 1938.

1920–1923: Rescuing the Bell and Searching for a Home

After the celebration, Ruschenberger and her fellow suffragists wanted the Justice Bell to remain in Independence Square, believing it deserved a place of national prominence. In 1921, several architects offered to design a "Citizenship Tower" to house the Justice Bell in Independence Square, where it had remained since the September 25 celebration. However, when Mayor J. Hampton Moore saw two soldiers salute the Justice Bell—something many soldiers commonly did for the Liberty Bell—he became so enraged that he ordered it to be destroyed. The bell was carted off to League Island Park in South Philadelphia and placed in a warehouse that doubled as a slaughterhouse and sheep-shearing station.

On July 4, 1923, the Justice Bell returned to Independence Square for a celebration. Afterward, it was transported to a grove in Valley Forge, where Reverend W. Herbert Burk, rector of the Washington Memorial Chapel, accepted it and had it placed in the woods near the chapel.[1]

1924: A Get Out the Vote Caravan

In 1924, the Justice Bell was put into service again when Katharine Wentworth Ruschenberger and other members of the Pennsylvania League of Women Voters embarked on a one-month, thirty-nine-county tour as part of a Get Out the Vote campaign. Their goal was to encourage voter registration and participation in the upcoming November 4 election. They aimed to increase voter turnout in Pennsylvania by 25 percent over the 1920 totals, when only 42 percent of eligible voters cast ballots. Their motto was "Vote as you please, but vote."

On October 1, 1924, women gathered at Independence Square in Philadelphia to hear speeches from Mayor W. Freeland Hendricks; Lucy Kennedy Miller, now chair of the Pennsylvania League of Women Voters; and Charlotte Augusta Brown Lea (Mrs. Charles M. Lea) of Devon, the director of the caravan. As they listened, airplanes from the Navy Yard dropped patriotic leaflets on the crowd. After the speeches, between 150 and 200 decorated cars set off on the journey, with the Justice Bell leading the convoy.[2]

Throughout the trip, local caravans joined the Justice Bell and the women as they entered each county. Ruschenberger and Mary Sleichter, both veterans of the 1915 campaign, remained with the caravan for the entire tour, while other women participated for shorter periods. Among those involved were Henrietta Baldy Lyon from Lycoming County, Lucy Kennedy Miller from Allegheny County, and Margaret Blackburn from Cumberland County. On October 5, Mary Lippincott of Wyncote arrived in Harrisburg to replace Charlotte Augusta Brown Lea as director of the tour. Martha Gibbons Thomas, treasurer for the Pennsylvania League of Women Voters and state representative for District 2, also participated in the tour. She was one of eight women elected to the Pennsylvania House of Representatives in 1922.

During the campaign, the women emphasized the importance of voting, noting that in many elections, only a small percentage of eligible voters participated in choosing their representatives. In 1920, for instance, only 1,852,616 Pennsylvanians—less than half of those eligible—cast ballots. In a speech quoted in the *Pottsville Republican* on October 3, 1924, Mary James Vaux (Mrs. George Vaux) of Bryn Mawr stated, "In 1920 there were four million eligible voters in the State, and less than half of this number cast their ballots." She added that at least eight thousand women in Schuylkill County were eligible to vote in the upcoming election, yet only two thousand had registered.[3]

Lucy Kennedy Miller was quoted at length on October 16, 1924, in the *Brookville American*, a newspaper of Jefferson County:

> Do we want to have our governmental institutions drift into the control of a small minority of the whole number of citizens? Of course not, but we should thoroughly appreciate the fact that in times of peace the security of the Republic rests upon the foundation of active citizenship. If the indications are that this foundation is tending toward weakness, it is the duty of the patriot to strengthen it. The object of the "Get-out-the-Vote" Campaign and of the Caravan of the Pennsylvania League of Women Voters is to strengthen the foundation of active citizenship.
>
> Since 1896, the number of eligible voters who cast their ballots has been steadily decreasing . . . . In 1920, less than 50 per cent cast ballots. Reflect on this: if less than 50 per cent of

> the voters go to the polls, then it is possible for 25 per cent of the eligible voters to constitute a majority and control the elections and therefore, the government. If we want to get rid of "borers-from-within," that is those who count on winning control by a so-called peaceful revolution, then we must support the "Get-out-the-Vote" Campaign which is inspired from start to finish by love of country.
>
> Four years ago, in this State, there were 4,330,348 possible voting citizens. The total vote was 1,852,616 or about 43 per cent of the possible voting strength. In short, a small minority of the citizens of Pennsylvania decided, four years ago, how Pennsylvania's vote should be cast in the Electoral College. This was because 2,477,732 citizens sat by the fire. The country needs more men and women who are willing to go out into the open and proclaim their citizenship.
>
> Two years ago, in the election of the Governor, and of other state officials, the total vote cast was only 1,464,603 or 34 per cent of the voting population. The total vote in the primary election, when the candidates for Governor were nominated, was even smaller: 1,207,920. In other words, only about 28 per cent of the voting population took part in the primaries and it should be remembered that, practically, the result of the November election, in that instance, as in many others in Pennsylvania, was determined by a majority of 28 per cent, so to speak, or about 15 per cent. Instead of having our affairs of state decided by a majority of all citizens, they were decided by an absolute minority of 15 per cent. These statistics are recited, of course, without regard to personalities. No earnest member of any party or of any faction sincerely desires a continuance of such minority decisions.[4]

The 1924 total showed improvement, with 2,144,850 people casting their ballots—262,234 more than in 1920.

After the tour, the Justice Bell was returned to the care of Rev. Burk, who again placed it in the woods near the chapel. Over the next fourteen years, the Justice Bell, once a powerful symbol of the movement, lapsed into obscurity. When Rev. Burk died in 1933, the bell was still not publicly displayed. Over the next several decades, the Justice Bell remained abandoned in the woods, as Burk's successors showed no interest in it.

On February 28, 1936, Ruschenberger wrote her Last Will and Testament, in which she transferred ownership of the Justice Bell to the Provident Trust Company of Philadelphia.

> Whereas I am the owner of the replica of the Liberty Bell, now known as the Justice Bell . . . [i]t is my desire to make such disposition of this bell as will continuously follow the purpose for which it was cast, namely, to become the symbol of the aim and ideal of the Constitution of the United States of America to "establish justice"; I do give and bequeath the said "Justice Bell," which is now at Valley Forge, to Provident Trust Company of Philadelphia, its successors and assigns, in Trust nevertheless to permit the same to be held by such prominent or historic organizations as in its soul and absolute discretion it may from time to time deem best, it being my intent and purpose that it shall at all times be in a place where it can be viewed by the public at large, my preference being that the Bell remain permanently at Valley Forge.
>
> And I do give and request unto Provident Trust Company of Philadelphia, its successors and assigns, the sum of twenty-five hundred dollars ($2,500) to be held in Trust by it perpetually to pay the net income therefrom to the custodian for the time being of the above-described bell. The said net income shall be used by the recipient thereof, first, for the cost of insurance, maintenance, and repairs of and to the said bell and, secondly, for the general use and purposes of such organization as shall receive the same.[5]

1938: The Justice Bell Is Abandoned in the Woods

In 1938, Ruschenberger once again searched for a place of national prominence where the Justice Bell could be displayed. Her efforts were to no avail. Nobody was interested. And without the attention that such a placement would have afforded, people soon forgot about the once-famous bell. When Katharine Wentworth Ruschenberger passed away on February 11, 1943, the Justice Bell was left abandoned in the woods, which is where it remained for the following five decades.

1992: The Justice Bell Is Rediscovered

In 1992, the Washington Memorial Chapel hired a new rector, Rev. Richard Lyon Stinson. When he came upon the bell in the woods and realized its significance, he contacted the Pennsylvania League of Women Voters and began taking steps for it to be moved into the chapel's bell tower.

1995–1997: The Justice Bell Receives Renewed Attention

On April 25, 1995, the Pennsylvania League of Women Voters took the Justice Bell on a four-month tour to celebrate the League's seventy-fifth anniversary. League members Sallie Corbishley, Anne Suss, and Mary Belle Ball accompanied the bell, which made its first stop in Harrisburg. As Corbishley told the *Philadelphia Inquirer*, "The trip's purpose is to celebrate the passage of the 19th Amendment and remind people that these suffragettes worked more than 50 years to get women the right to vote."[6]

The Justice Bell spent a week in the rotunda of the state capitol before being moved on May 1 to the State Museum in Harrisburg, where it remained on display through May 24. On August 22, 1995, the Justice Bell was returned to the Washington Memorial Chapel, and four days later the League celebrated the seventy-fifth anniversary of the Nineteenth Amendment with a Ratification Day picnic at the chapel.

In October, the bell was taken to Philadelphia for a five-month exhibition at Independence National Historical Park. Afterward, it underwent more than four months of repairs while architect David E. Freeman of King of Prussia, Pennsylvania, designed a new base to provide structural support so the bell could be rung. The Florig Equipment Company reinforced the wooden platform with a steel structure and handled the bell's transport from Philadelphia back to the Washington Memorial Chapel.

On August 22, 1996, the Justice Bell was placed in the rotunda at the base of the chapel's bell tower. The League of Women Voters gathered for another Ratification Day picnic to celebrate the return of the Justice Bell. Rev. Richard Lyon Stinson led the festivities.

On August 26, 1997, Pennsylvania's Lieutenant Governor Mark Schweiker spoke at the Washington Memorial Chapel during a ceremony rededicating the Justice Bell and commemorating the seventy-seventh anniversary of the Nineteenth Amendment.[7] Another seven years would pass before the bell received public attention once again.

2004: A Bell-to-Bell Bike Ride

In 2004, to celebrate the eighty-fifth anniversary of Pennsylvania's ratification of the Nineteenth Amendment on June 24, 1919, the Valley Forge Convention and Visitors Bureau, under the direction of Linda Riley, Director of Communications, and Renee Amoore, honorary chair of Women Advancing—a region-wide initiative celebrating women's voices and voting rights—sponsored a twenty-two-mile bike ride along the Schuylkill River Trail, from the Liberty Bell to the Justice Bell. Joan Hanscom, the event director of Threshold Sports, helped organize the event, which took place on Sunday, June 27, 2004. Women Advancing made it their signature event and handled the registrations. Actresses portraying Abigail Adams, Sojourner Truth, and other historical women greeted the riders at both bell locations.[8]

The event was a success, but it did not sustain public awareness of the Justice Bell. For another eleven years, the bell remained largely forgotten.

2015–2016: Steps Toward Recognition

In 2015, the centennial of both the Justice Bell's creation and its historic tour of Pennsylvania, two public events marked meaningful steps toward renewed recognition of the bell and its place in the women's suffrage movement.

From August 5 to October 31, 2015, an exhibit at Independence National Historical Park (INHP) in Philadelphia, titled *Independence Hall and Votes for Women*, featured the story of the Justice Bell. The idea for the exhibit, along with most of the research, came from Holly Holst, a park ranger at INHP.[9]

On September 13, 2015, the League of Women Voters and the National Society of the Daughters of the American Revolution (DAR) hosted a ceremonial re-chaining of the bell's clapper at the Washington Memorial Chapel.

A year later, on August 31, 2016, Amanda Owen, this book's author, and Mingo Stroeber founded the Justice Bell Foundation with the goal of raising awareness of the Justice Bell's historic role in the American women's suffrage movement. The foundation developed programs for adults and children, created a Justice Bell replica that could tour throughout Pennsylvania, and produced a documentary about the bell.

Even so, while the exhibition, commemoration, and a new organization marked a meaningful return of the bell to the public's awareness, the years ahead would underscore how easily history can fade without sustained attention, and how urgent the work of stewardship remains.

2020: The Justice Bell Falls Off a Truck and Is Damaged

On August 25, 2020, workers from the Mammoet Company loaded the Justice Bell onto a flatbed truck at the Washington Memorial Chapel for transport to Independence Square in Philadelphia. The bell was to appear the following day at a ceremony marking the centennial of the Nineteenth Amendment. But as the truck rounded its first curve, the bell—improperly secured—fell onto the road. Chunks of metal broke off the lip, the clapper and yoke were damaged, and the carriage and platform were destroyed.

The workers managed to get the bell back onto the truck and deliver it to Philadelphia, where it was placed on the ground on pieces of wood for the ceremony, a sparsely attended event due to the COVID-19 pandemic.

Days later, the bell disappeared from public view. Representatives from the Washington Memorial Chapel offered no explanation about what had happened, its condition, or its whereabouts. Repeated inquiries over the ensuing years yielded only vague and shifting answers: the bell would be back in two months, or by spring, or summer, or when insurance issues were settled. No one would say where it was, what had happened, or what repairs, if any, were underway.

In late 2021, the Justice Bell Foundation discovered that the bell had been sent to Cincinnati, Ohio, to the Verdin Company, a business that manufactures and restores bells. Still, there were no updates or public statements about its condition or plans for its return. Two more years passed.

On June 5, 2023, the Justice Bell Foundation contacted the Verdin Company to ask about the bell's condition and its return, but was referred back to the chapel, which did not respond to an inquiry. Two months later, on August 2, 2023, without public notice, the bell reappeared at the Washington Memorial Chapel, according to a post on the chapel's Facebook page. Photographs showed the bell looking visibly worse for wear: streaks

The Justice Bell at the Washington Memorial Chapel, August 29, 2023.

marked its surface, chips were visible along the lip, and its once-polished patina finish had dulled.

On August 12, 2023, Tim Verdin confirmed to the Justice Bell Foundation that on August 25, 2020, the bell, its clapper, and the yoke had been damaged and that the platform, carriage, and one of the A-stands had been destroyed. The second A-stand had a significant crack.

He described repairs to three locations on the bell's lip where chunks had broken off and explained that microfractures had been welded along the lip. The clapper was also welded. He said the bell's dull surface and streaked appearance were due to acid solutions applied to the bell in order to conduct X-ray and magnetic particle testing for cracks in the metal. Although the bell had developed a beautiful natural patina over more than a century, Verdin explained that its previously polished appearance resulted from the accumulation of dirt and oils left by people touching it, and that it would regain that sheen as more people continued to handle it.

Verdin's remarks offered a technical perspective, but the bell's condition also raised broader questions about how we care for historical objects and the stories they carry.

Despite everything, the Justice Bell is still here. It has been lost, damaged, ignored, and forgotten—and still it survives. That survival is not due to luck. It is due to the persistence of those who keep asking where it is, what it means, and how it should be remembered. In the end, the legacy of the Justice Bell will rest with those who continue to safeguard its story, just as the future of all historic objects is sustained by those who choose to protect and honor them.

Afterword

Securing the Legacy of the Justice Bell (2015–2025)

What started as an effort to document a single symbol grew into a broader journey of preservation. Because much of the Justice Bell's history had never been chronicled, I approached this book eager to provide a narrative based on the information I had collected over several years of research. Through the writing process, additional information emerged, filling gaps in the bell's story and shedding light on the vital role Pennsylvania women played in the larger struggle for women's voting rights in early twentieth-century America.

Long before I began writing, I had committed to ensuring that this history would not be forgotten again. In 2016, I cofounded the Justice Bell Foundation to reintroduce the Justice Bell to the public. In 2019, the Justice Bell Foundation collaborated with the Pennsylvania Academy of the Fine Arts to create a Justice Bell replica that travels to libraries, historical societies, and other institutions. That same year, we helped secure official recognition of the bell's contribution through Pennsylvania Senate Resolution 405, which entered its history into the public record for the first time. In 2020, the Justice Bell Foundation and Wild West Women, Inc. produced my documentary, *Finding Justice: The Untold Story of Women's Fight for the Vote.*

In 2024, the Justice Bell Foundation partnered with Montgomery County Community College (MCCC) in Blue Bell, Pennsylvania, to establish the first official Justice Bell archive to serve as the offical repository for the Justice Bell's historical documention. The archive includes two collections: a 1915 collection with material related to the bell's twentieth century travels, and a 2015 collection with more recent records fom the Justice Bell Foundation. These materials are accessible to the college community and the public from MCCC's Archive & Special Collections in the Brendlinger Library on the Blue Bell Campus. As part of the archive, our Justice Bell replica has a permanent home there when it is not being exhibited at other locations. The original Justice Bell continues to be housed at the Washington Memorial Chapel.

There is still more to uncover. Descendants remain to be traced, photographs may yet surface, and local histories could hold vital fragments of the story. I hope this book provides a foundation for others to build upon. More than a century after the Justice Bell captured the nation's attention, it is more important than ever that women's achievements and symbols are neither forgotten nor erased. The silence that once surrounded the Justice Bell reminds us how easily history can be lost—not because it lacks significance, but because it was not preserved.

It has been an honor to help reclaim this story and to follow in the footsteps of the women who believed justice was worth the fight. Their determination and vision still resonate, and I am grateful for the opportunity to help ensure that their legacy endures.

Acknowledgments

I am indebted to those who preserved women's history during the early twentieth century by documenting what women were actually doing—activities absent from most history books. Their work gave me a foothold as I began what became a years-long research project. Because of them, I was able to piece together the story I tell in this book about the suffragists who so brilliantly made use of a symbol for equality and voting rights.

I am especially beholden to Henrietta Louise Krone for her dissertation, "Dauntless Women: The Story of the Woman Suffrage Movement in Pennsylvania, 1910–20," completed in 1946; and Caroline Katzenstein for her firsthand account of the Pennsylvania women's suffrage movement in her book *Lifting the Curtain: The State and National Woman Suffrage Campaigns in Pennsylvania As I Saw Them*, published in 1955.

Online resources also proved essential. Newspaper accounts helped me document the bell's journey, and Alexander Street offered crowdsourced biographies of many of the suffragists who participated in the campaign.

Over the years, I reached out to individuals who had been involved with the Justice Bell at various times in its history. I thank Reverend Richard Lyon Stinson, former rector at the Washington Memorial Chapel, not only for rescuing the bell from the woods, but also for giving so generously of his time to me during multiple interviews. I am indebted to Sallie Corbishley, who provided me with important information about her discovery of the photographs of the 1915 tour and shared details about the 1995 tour, in which she participated. Linda Riley, one of the organizers of the 2004 bell-to-bell bike ride, met with me in 2016 and provided information about that event. I am grateful.

I also thank the following people who helped me fill in details about the suffragists:

Sandi Tatnall, great-niece of Katharine Ruschenberger, spoke with me about her great-aunt and has been instrumental in preserving her great-aunt's legacy.

Information about Louise Hall's contributions came from several sources. Elisa Miller, department chair and associate professor of history at Rhode Island College, shared her article "Uncovering the Lives of Ordinary Rhode Island Suffragists" and her biography of Hall on Alexander Street. Craig Walker, a historian for the Ojai Valley Museum in Ojai, California, provided information about Hall's life in Ojai after she and Ethel Bret Harte moved there in the 1930s. Linda Texter Hall, whose husband Roger Hall was Louise Hall's nephew, contributed invaluable firsthand information, along with a comprehensive genealogy from her family's personal papers.

Thanks to Coleen Smith, archivist for the Association of MIT Alumnae, for her diligence in tracking down Oliver Hall's suffragist credentials and confirming his participation in the Boston parade prior to the Justice Bell tour.

I thank James Merrick, archivist at the Stanley Museum, for his research on the bell truck, which confirmed its make and model.

I also thank Amy Ensley, M.S., former director of the Hankey Center for the History of Women's Education at Wilson College in Chambersburg, Pennsylvania, for her work documenting Hannah Patterson's life and achievements; and Jennifer Hurl, archivist at the Meyersdale Public Library in Meyersdale, Pennsylvania, for documenting Alice Kiernan's contributions.

Many thanks to Janet Lindenmuth, law librarian at Widener University Delaware Law School, who took on the task of documenting Rose Winslow (Ruza Wenclawska). After seeing the Broadway show *Suffs*, Lindenmuth was appalled to learn how little was known about Winslow, a featured figure in the musical, including the location of her burial. She resolved to uncover the facts and publish her findings. Her article, "Ruza Wenclawska: Suffragist, Labor Organizer, Poet and Actor," can be found on her website.

I am also grateful to the many individuals working at historical societies throughout Pennsylvania who gave generously of their time and expertise, often providing undigitized information and archival materials that I have incorporated into this book. They include Rose Marie Kendall, secretary of the board at the Beaver County Genealogy and History Center; Margaret Skrivseth, executive director of the Huntingdon County Historical Society; Nancy Spencer of the Sullivan County Historical Society; and Mary L. Sieminksi, retired librarian and project manager for the Lycoming County Women's History Project, an online archive of source material relating to the history of women in Lycoming County, Pennsylvania.

For assistance with York County suffragists and the Justice Bell tour, I thank June Burk Lloyd, librarian emerita at the York County History Center, and Samantha Dorm, York County History Center board member and cofounder of the Friends of Lebanon Cemetery. Bernadine Lennon, treasurer and chair of the Greene-Dreher Historical Society Research Committee in Greentown, Pennsylvania, searched the archives and found undigitized materials about the Justice Bell's tour through Pike, Wayne, and Monroe Counties. Thanks to Dorothy Gruskowski for information related to the Monongahela River ferry service between Greene and Fayette Counties. Thanks as well to Christina Larocco, member of the Editorial Advisory Committee at the Historical Society of Pennsylvania, who provided access to newspapers documenting Alice Dunbar-Nelson's activities.

Researchers at the Elk County, Cameron County, and Schuylkill County historical societies combed through their archives to locate information about the Justice Bell and confirmed that it did not travel through their counties in 1915. I am grateful to Susan Hoy, vice president of the Cameron County Historical Society; Nancy Peterson, director of the Elk County Historical Society; and Lee Singer, research library volunteer at the Schuylkill County Historical Society.

Photographs in this book came from a variety of sources. I am grateful to the Schlesinger Library at the Radcliffe Institute, Harvard University, for the papers of Ethel Bret Harte and Elizabeth McShane; the Historical Society of Pennsylvania, for the League of Women Voters photographs donated by Sallie Corbishley; the Cumberland County Historical Society, for a photograph of the bell in Carlisle; and Michael Trump, for his photograph of the suffragists with the bell in Lebanon County. I am also grateful to Kenneth Florey for his photograph of the plaster bell featured in the 1913 Erie Perry Centennial parade, and to Eliza Smith Brown, great-niece of Lucy Kennedy Miller, for her photograph of Miller. Additional photographs came from Temple University, the Pennsylvania State Archives, and the Library of Congress, and I am grateful for their contributions.

For editorial assistance and feedback, I thank Marcelline Krafchick, Linda Texter Hall, and Lisa K. Manwill Marietta. Many thanks to Jeff Witchel, Adobe InDesign teacher extraordinare, who taught me how to design the book you hold in your hands.

On a personal note, many thanks to Lori Morse-Dolan, Justice Bell Foundation advisory board member, for her unwavering support for this book project and for her help locating information about Augusta Fleming; Linda Texter Hall who read an early version of this manuscript and offered helpful suggestions; Nicole Maugle, Director of Libraries at Montgomery County Community College, who has championed the story of the Justice Bell and helped bring this book to publication; and Martha Wheelock, Justice Bell Foundation board member, for her dedication to documenting women's history through teaching, writing, and filmmaking, for her invaluable feedback and encouragement over the years I worked on this manuscript, and for her friendship.

Lastly, I thank The Joans C., Marian D., and Robert H. Erb Charitable Fund (Erb Fund) for funding the first print runs of both this book and the forthcoming children's book, both of which will become part of the Justice Bell Archive & Special Collections at Montgomery County Community College in Blue Bell, Pennsylvania. Learn more about the archive at mc3.edu/JusticeBell.

Discussion Guide

The Justice Bell: Tracing the Journey of a Forgotten Symbol
By Amanda Owen

Use these questions to spark conversation in book clubs, classrooms, or community groups.

Historical Themes

1. What surprised you most about the history of the Justice Bell? Why do you think this symbol has been largely forgotten?
2. How did the Justice Bell campaign reflect the political strategies and social dynamics of the women's suffrage movement?
3. In what way did the Justice Bell campaign both reflect and challenge the norms of its time regarding women's visibility in public life and politics?

Symbols and Legacy

4. How did the use of a physical object like the Justice Bell shape public engagement with the suffrage movement? What does this suggest about the power of symbolism in political activism?
5. How does the Justice Bell compare to other historic American symbols, such as the Liberty Bell? What does it represent today?
6. What is the significance of silence in the Justice Bell's story? How did that silence convey a message then and now?

Personal Connections

6. Did reading about the Justice Bell change the way you think about women's rights or civic participation?
7. What parallels can you draw between the Justice Bell campaign and current efforts for equality and representation?
8. What role do symbols play in modern movements for social change?

Applying the Lessons

9. If you were to design a campaign today using a symbol like the Justice Bell, what would it look like? Could the Justice Bell serve as a symbol for equality and voting rights today?
10. What actions can individuals or communities take to preserve and share overlooked stories like this one?

To access additional resources or inquire about virtual visits, screenings, or classroom presentations, visit www.justicebell.org.

Further Reading

The Pennsylvania Women's Suffrage Movement

Harper, Ida Husted, ed. *The History of Woman Suffrage*. Vol. 6, 1900–1920, pp. 550–64. New York: National American Woman Suffrage Association, 1922.

Katzenstein, Caroline. *Lifting the Curtain: The State and National Woman Suffrage Campaigns in Pennsylvania as I Saw Them*. Philadelphia: Dorrance & Company, Inc., 1955.

Krone, Henrietta Louise. *Dauntless Women: The Story of the Woman Suffrage Movement in Pennsylvania, 1910–20*. PhD diss., University of Pennsylvania, Philadelphia, PA, 1946.

Young, Robyn S. *Women's Suffrage in Pennsylvania: 1840–1920*. Queen's Perch Press, LLC., Media, Pennsylvania, 1925.

Women's Suffrage Movement in the United States

Baker, Jean H., *Sisters: The Lives of America's Suffragists*. New York: Hill and Wang, 2006.

Catt, Carrie Chapman, and Nettie Rogers Shuler. *Woman Suffrage and Politics: The Inner Story of the Suffrage Movement*. New York: Dover Publications, 2020.

Cooney, Robert P., Jr. *Winning the Vote: The Triumph of the American Woman Suffrage Movement*. Santa Cruz, CA: American Graphic Press, 2005.

DuBois, Ellen Carol. *Suffrage: Women's Long Battle for the Vote*. New York: Simon & Schuster, 2020.

Florey, Kenneth. *American Woman Suffrage Postcards: A Study and Catalog*. Jefferson, NC: McFarland & Company, 2015.

Harper, Ida Husted, et al. *History of Woman Suffrage*. Vol. 6, 1900–1920. New York: National American Woman Suffrage Association, 1922.

Lange, Allison K. *Picturing Political Power: Images in the Women's Suffrage Movement*. Chicago: University of Chicago Press, 2020.

Marino, Kelly L. *Votes for College Women: Alumni, Students, and the Woman Suffrage Campaign*. New York: NYU Press, 2024.

Rouse, Wendy L. *Public Faces, Secret Lives: A Queer History of the Women's Suffrage Movement*. New York: NYU Press, 2024.

Spruill, Marjorie J. ed. *One Woman, One Vote: Rediscovering the Woman Suffrage Movement*. 2nd ed. Tillamook, OR: NewSage Press, 2021.

Stevens, Doris. *Jailed for Freedom: American Women Win the Vote*. Edited by Carol O'Hare. Troutdale, OR: NewSage Press, 1995.

Wagner, Sallie Roesch. *The Women's Suffrage Movement*. New York: Penguin Classics, 2019.

Wagner, Sally Roesch. *Sisters in Spirit: Haudenosaunee (Iroquois) Influence on Early American Feminists*. Illustrated by John Fadden. Summertown, TN: Native Voices, 2001.

Ware, Susan. *Why They Marched: Untold Stories of the Women Who Fought for the Right to Vote*. Boston: Belknap Press, An Imprint of Harvard University Press, 2019.

Wayne, Tiffany K. *Women's Suffrage: The Complete Guide to the Nineteenth Amendment*. New York: ABC-CLIO, 2020.

Weiss, Elaine. *The Woman's Hour: The Great Fight to Win the Vote*. New York: Viking, 2018.

Black Women and the Women's Suffrage Movement

Cahill, Cathleen D. *Recasting the Vote: How Women of Color Transformed the Suffrage Movement*. Chapel Hill: University of North Carolina Press, 2020.

Dionne, Evette. *Lifting As We Climb: Black Women's Battle for the Ballot Box*. New York: Viking Books for Young Readers, 2020.

Dudden Faye E. *Fighting Chance: The Struggle Over Woman Suffrage and Black Suffrage in Reconstruction America*. New York: Oxford University Press, 2011.

Jones, Martha S. *Vanguard: How Black Women Broke Barriers, Won the Vote, and Insisted on Equality for All*. New York: Basic Books, 2020.

Terborg-Penn, Rosalyn. *African American Women in the Struggle for the Vote, 1850–1920*. Bloomington: Indiana University Press, 1998.

Biographies About Suffragists

Alexander, Eleanor. *Lyrics of Sunshine and Shadow: The Tragic Courtship and Marriage of Paul Laurence Dunbar and Alice Ruth Moore*. New York: NYU Press, 2001.

Brown, Eliza Smith. *She Devils at the Door.* Pittsburgh: Carnegie Mellon University Press, 2023.

Clinton, Catherine. *Harriet Tubman: The Road to Freedom.* New York: Little Brown and Company, 2004.

Duster, Michelle. *Ida B. Wells, Voice of Truth: Educator, Feminist, and Anti-Lynching Civil Rights Leader.* New York: Godwin Books, 2022.

Faulkner, Carol. *Lucretia Mott's Heresy: Abolition and Women's Rights in Nineteenth-Century America.* Philadelphia: University of Pennsylvania Press, 2013.

Green, Tara T. *Love, Activism, and the Respectable Life of Alice Dunbar-Nelson.* New York: Bloomsbury Academic, 2022.

Hamlin, Kimberly A. *Free Thinker: Sex, Suffrage, and the Extraordinary Life of Helen Hamilton Gardener.* New Yok: W. W. Norton & Company, 2020.

Hess, Kimberly. *A Lesser Mortal: The Unexpected Life of Sarah B. Cochran.* Nashville: Books Fluent, 2021.

Lewandowski, Tadeusz. *Red Bird, Red Power: The Life and Legacy of Zitkala-Ša* Vol. 67, American Indian Literature and Critical Studies Series. Oklahoma: University of Oklahoma Press, 2016.

Parker, Alison M. *Unceasing Militant: The Life of Mary Church Terrell.* Chapel Hill: University of North Carolina Press, 2020.

Rooks, Noliwe. *A Passionate Mind in Relentless Pursuit: The Vision of Mary McLeod Bethune.* Series edited by Henry Louis Gates Jr. New York: Penguin Press, 2024.

Walton, Mary. *A Woman's Crusade: Alice Paul and the Battle for the Ballot.* New York: St. Martin's Press, 2010.

Wickenden. *The Agitators: Three Friends Who Fought for Abolition and Women's Rights.* New York: Scribner, 2022.

Books About the History of Voting

Keyssar, Alexander. *The Right to Vote: The Contested History of Democracy in the United States.* New York: Basic Books, 2000.

Smith, Erin Geiger. *Thank You for Voting: The Maddening, Enlightening, Inspiring Truth About Voting in America.* New York: Harper, 2020.

Children's Books

Conkling, Winifred. *Votes for Women! American Suffragists and the Battle for the Ballot.* Illustrated edition. New York: Algonquin Young Readers, 2018.

Diesen, Deborah. *Equality's Call: The Story of Voting Rights in America.* Illustrated by Magdalena Mora. New York: Beach Lane Books, 2020.

Dionne, Evette. *Lifting As We Climb: Black Women's Battle for the Ballot Box.* Illustrated edition. New York: Viking Books for Young Readers, 2020.

Duster, Michele. *Ida B. Wells, Voice of Truth: Educator, Feminist, and Anti-Lynching Civil Rights Leader.* New York: Godwin Books, 2022.

Greenfield, Eloise. *Mary McLeod Bethune.* Illustrated by Jerry Pinkney. Crowell Biographies. New York: HarperCollins, 1994.

Kennedy, Nancy. *Women Win the Vote! 19 for the 19th Amendment.* Illustrated by Katy Dockrill. New York: Norton Young Readers; W. W. Norton & Company, 2020.

Kulling, Monica. *Susan B. Anthony: Her Fight for Equal Rights.* Illustrated by Maike Plenzke. Step into Reading. New York: Random House Books for Young Readers, 2020.

Messner, Kate. *History Smashers: Women's Right to Vote.* Illustrated by Dylan Meconis. New York: Random House Books for Young Readers, 2020.

Rockliff, Mara. *Around America to Win the Vote: Two Suffragists, a Kitten, and 10,000 Miles.* Somerville, MA: Candlewick Press, 2016.

Smith, Erin Geiger. *Thank You for Voting Young Readers' Edition: The Past, Present, and Future of Voting.* New York: Quill Tree Books, 2021.

Weiss, Elaine. *The Woman's Hour (Adapted for Young Readers): Our Fight for the Right to Vote.* New York: Random House Books for Young Readers, 2020.

Zimet, Susan, and Todd Hasak-Lowy. *Roses and Radicals: The Epic Story of How American Women Won the Right to Vote.* New York: Viking Books for Young Readers, 2018.

Notes

PART ONE
A Brief History

1 An individual's property, which included land and possessions, had to have a combined value of fifty pounds.

2 "How Did the Vote Expand?: New Jersey's Revolutionary Decade," Part 2 of *When Women Lost the Vote: A Revolutionary Story, 1776–1807*, a virtual exhibit of the Museum of the American Revolution, Philadelphia, PA. Online at https://www.amrevmuseum.org/virtualexhibits/when-women-lost-the-vote-a-revolutionary-story/pages/how-did-the-vote-expand-new-jersey-s-revolutionary-decade.

3 Henrietta Louise Krone, "Dauntless Women: The Story of the Woman Suffrage Movement in Pennsylvania, 1910–20" (PhD diss., University of Pennsylvania, 1946).

4 "Suffrage Wins Sudden Victory in the Senate: To Surprise of Both Sides, Proposition for Popular Vote Is Endorsed: M'Nichols Turns the Tide," *Pittsburgh Post*, April 23, 1913.

5 "Hannah J. Patterson: Feminist Trailblazer: The Campaign in Pennsylvania in 1914." A virtual exhibit of the Hankey Center & C. Elizabeth Boyd '33 Archives. Wilson College. Chambersburg, PA.

6 Jennie Bradley Roessing Papers, 1887–1962, AIS.1964.24, Archives & Special Collections, University of Pittsburgh Library System.

7 Henrietta Louise Krone, "Dauntless Women: The Story of the Woman Suffrage Movement in Pennsylvania, 1910–20" (PhD diss., University of Pennsylvania, 1946).

8 Roberta J. Leach, "Jennie Bradley Roessing and the Fight for Woman Suffrage in Pennsylvania," *Western Pennsylvania Historical Magazine* 67 (July 1984).

9 "Suffrage Bell Arrives Today: Advocates of Votes for Women Plan a Hearty Welcome for It," *Daily Local News* (West Chester, PA), October 30, 1915.

10 "Suffrage Leaders Plan Campaign to Enlist Men in Fight for the Ballot," *Scranton (PA) Truth*, November 19, 1914.

11 Elisa Miller, "Uncovering the Lives of Ordinary Rhode Island Suffragists," *The Bridge: A Joint Edition of the Journals of Newport History and Rhode Island History* (Fall 2020): 19–45.

12 "Suffragists Solve Question of Dress for Votes Pageant: Marchers Decide to Wear Dark Skirts and Yellow Sashes and Carry Oriental Lanterns: More Speakers Coming: Washington Woman and 'Suffrage Beauty' to Help Deliver Final Blows for Vote," *Evening Public Ledger* (Philadelphia PA), October 14, 1915.

13 "Miss Louise Hall," *The Republic* (Meyersdale, PA), July 29, 1915.

14 "Biographical Sketch of Louise Hall," by Elisa Miller. Included in Part III: Mainstream Suffragists—National American Woman Suffrage Association. Alexander Street, part of Clarivate.

15 Harriet Ellsworth Siebert, *Ancestors and Descendants of Chief Justice Oliver Ellsworth and His Wife, Abigail Wolcott*, December 25, 1940, 21–22 of 77 pages, family document, courtesy of Linda Texter Hall from her family papers; Linda Texter Hall (descendant by marriage to Roger Wolcott Hall, nephew of Louise Hall), interviews with the author, 2019–2024.

16 "Suffrage Leaders Call Big Rally: Party Lieutenants from All Parts of State Will Meet in Harrisburg on April 8th," *Allentown (PA) Democrat*, April 2, 1915.

17 "Biographical Sketch of Katharine Wentworth Ruschenberger," written by Laurie A. Rofini. Included in Part III: Mainstream Suffragists—National American Woman Suffrage Association. Alexander Street, part of Clarivate.

18 Laurie A. Rofini. "Rung It Never Can Be Until All Women Are Free: Katharine Wentworth Ruschenberger and the Justice Bell," *Pennsylvania History: A Journal of Mid-Atlantic Studies* 87, no. 4 (Autumn 2020), Penn State University Press.

19 Henrietta Louise Krone, "Dauntless Women: The Story of the Woman Suffrage Movement in Pennsylvania, 1910–20" (PhD diss., University of Pennsylvania, 1946), pp. 83–84.

20 Henrietta Louise Krone, "Dauntless Women: The Story of the Woman Suffrage Movement in Pennsylvania, 1910–20" (PhD diss., University of Pennsylvania, 1946), 88.

21 Henrietta Louise Krone, "Dauntless Women: The Story of the Woman Suffrage Movement in Pennsylvania, 1910–20" (PhD diss., University of Pennsylvania, 1946), 97–99.

22 "Suffragists Visit Independence Hall Before Trip," *Evening Public Ledger* (Philadelphia, PA), March 30, 1915.

23 "Little Suffragist to Cast the Women's Liberty Bell," *Harrisburg (PA) Telegraph*, March 31, 1915.

24 "Casting of Liberty Bell in the Movies," *Tribune* (Scranton, PA), April 7, 1915.

25 "Mrs. Katharine Wentworth Ruschenberger," *Delaware County Daily Times* (Chester, PA), April 1, 1915.

PART TWO
The 1915 Justice Bell Tour

1 "Do Stout Ladies Want the Vote? Ask Mrs. Grusel, Who Carried 200 Pounds of Suffrage Sentiment into Catawissa," *Mercersburg (PA) Journal*, October 1, 1915.

2 "Great Slashing of Ballots at the November Election: Mrs. DeGroot Elected a Member of the Board of Education; Mrs. Kohler Defeated by Three Votes—Numerous Changes Made in Town Council and Other Borough Offices," *Allentown (PA) Leader*, November 3, 1915.

3 "Appeals for Suffrage," *York (PA) Dispatch*, November 2, 1915.

4 "Suffrage Bell in Montgomery on Way Despite Rain," *Reading (PA) Times*, October 16, 1915.

5 "Suffrage Bell Coming to St. Mary's," *Daily Press* (St. Mary's, PA), July 14, 1915.

6 "Local Suffragettes Should Get Busy," *Daily Press* (St. Mary's, PA), June 19, 1915. Correspondence from historical societies in Elk, Cameron, and Schuylkill Counties affirms that there were no reports of the Justice Bell in their counties.

7 "Helen M. Todd," Wikipedia, last modified February 16, 2025.

8 Barry Popik, "'We want bread, but we want roses, too' (Bread and Roses Strike)," *The Big Apple* website, March 29, 2014.

9 "Helen Todd," *New York Daily News*, August 16, 1953.

10 "Biographical Sketch of Mary Moore Wolfe," by Christina Larocco.

Included in *Part III: Mainstream Suffragists—National American Woman Suffrage Association*. Alexander Street, part of Clarivate.

11 "Laurelton Village: The Home for Feeble-Minded Women," *Valley Girl Views*, Heather Truckenmiller's blog about the Central Susquehanna Valley, March 8, 2023.

12 "Eudora Ramsay Richardson (1891–1973)," by Andrea Ledesma, in *Dictionary of Virginia Biography*. Library of Virginia (1998–), published 2018.

13 "Biographical Sketch of Augusta Brown Fleming," by Katherine Pettine. Included in *Part III: Mainstream Suffragists—National American Woman Suffrage Association*. Alexander Street, part of Clarivate.

14 Kenneth Florey, *American Woman Suffrage Postcards: A Study and Catalog* (Jefferson, NC: McFarland & Company Inc., 2015).

15 "Suffrage Head Appeals to the Women of Erie," *Erie (PA) Daily Times*, July 6, 1913.

16 "Biographical Sketch of Augusta Brown Fleming," by Katherine Pettine. Included in *Part III: Mainstream Suffragists—National American Woman Suffrage Association*. Alexander Street, part of Clarivate.

17 "Mrs. Fleming, Former Civic Leader, Dies," *Erie (PA) Morning News*, July 25, 1949.

18 "Biographical Sketch of Mary Stewart," by Kelly Kirk. Included in *Part III: Mainstream Suffragists—National American Woman Suffrage Association*. Alexander Street, part of Clarivate.

19 "Liberty Bell Here Today: Roads in Bad Shape and the Progress Is Necessarily Slow," *Evening Republican* (Meadville, PA), June 30, 1915.

20 "History of the Collect for Clubwomen," GFWC Oregon Federation of Woman's Clubs, Oregon, https://oregongfwc.org/collect.html.

21 "Hannah Jane Patterson," in *Notable American Women, 1607–1950*, vol. 3, *P–Z* (Cambridge, MA: Belknap Press of Harvard University Press, 1971), 28–29.

22 Amy Ensley, "Hannah J. Patterson: Feminist Trailblazer," online exhibit, Hankey Center, Wilson College, 2021. Online at http://exhibits.wilson.edu/exhibits/show/hannah-j-patterson-feminist.

23 "Biographical Sketch of Lucy Kennedy Miller," by Christina Larocco. Included in *Part III: Mainstream Suffragists—National American Woman Suffrage Association*. Alexander Street, part of Clarivate.

24 Eliza Smith Brown, *She Devils at the Door* (Pittsburgh, PA: Carnegie Mellon University Press, 2023).

25 Elizabeth McShane Hilles suffrage and biographical information, 1909–1989. Papers of Elizabeth McShane Hilles, 1909-1989, A/H6521, 1. Schlesinger Library, Radcliffe Institute.

26 Elizabeth McShane Hilles suffrage and biographical information, 1909–1989. Papers of Elizabeth McShane Hilles, 1909-1989, A/H6521, 1. Schlesinger Library, Radcliffe Institute.

27 Elizabeth McShane Hilles suffrage and biographical information, 1909–1989. Papers of Elizabeth McShane Hilles, 1909-1989, A/H6521, 1. Schlesinger Library, Radcliffe Institute.

28 "Abuse and Ailments: Elizabeth McShane (1891–1976)," affidavit, signed and notarized November 28, 1917. National Woman's Party Records, Manuscript Division, Library of Congress (110.00.00).

29 "Biographical Sketch of Elizabeth McShane Hilles," by Jessica Roden. Included in *Part I: Militant Women Suffragists—National Woman's Party*. Database assembled and co-edited by Thomas Dublin and Kathryn Sklar. Biographical sketches have been crowdsourced. (Alexandria, VA: Alexander Street Press, 2015).

30 "Harriet Grim," Wikipedia, last modified March 9, 2024.

31 "Biographical Sketch of Harriet Elizabeth Grim," by John Bays and Nima Lane. Included in *Part III: Mainstream Suffragists—National American Woman Suffrage Association*, Alexander Street, part of Clarivate.

32 "Suffragists Insist on Plank in the National Party Platform," *Ottumwa (IA) Tri-Weekly Courier*, June 16, 1908.

33 "Harriet E. Grim, Retired Speech Professor, Dies," *Wisconsin State Journal*, September 9, 1967.

34 "Biographical Sketch of Emma Lenore MacAlarney," by Joshua Slater. Included in *Part III: Mainstream Suffragists—National American Woman Suffrage Association*. Alexander Street, part of Clarivate.

35 "Miss MacAlarney Interested Large Audience Last Night," *Daily Republican* (Phoenixville, PA), October 15, 1915.

36 "A Patriotic Love Feast," *Bedford (PA) Gazette*, August 6,1915.

37 "Biographical Sketch of Alice F. Kiernan," by Kimberly Drotar. Included in *Part I: Militant Women Suffragists—National Woman's Party*. Database assembled and co-edited by Thomas Dublin and Kathryn Sklar. Biographical sketches have been crowdsourced. Alexander Street Press (Alexandria, VA), 2015.

38 "Suffragists Had Big Demonstration," *Pittsburgh Press*, July 14, 1914.

39 Jennifer Baer Hurl, "West-Central PA Women's Suffrage: Somerset County," in *West-Central PA Women's Suffrage*, created by Dr. Barbara Zaborowski, Meyersdale Public Library, August 24, 2021. Online at https://

www.meyersdalelibrary.org/suffragist-project.

40 "Biographical Sketch of Susan Walker FitzGerald," by Lyle Nyberg. Included in *Part III: Mainstream Suffragists—National American Woman Suffrage Association*. Alexander Street, part of Clarivate.

41 "Mrs. Susan W. FitzGerald," *Hartford (CT) Courant*, January 21, 1943.

42 Coleen Smith (archivist for the Association of MIT Alumnae (AMITA), interview with the author, 2024.

43 Harriet Ellsworth Siebert, *Ancestors and Descendants of Chief Justice Oliver Ellsworth and His Wife, Abigail Wolcott*, December 25, 1940, pp. 21–22. Courtesy of Linda Texter Hall, from her family papers.

44 Oliver Cushing Hall, Roll: 1561893, Draft Board 1, Hartford, CT, in "World War I Draft Registration Cards, 1917–1918," Ancestry.com, accessed February 13, 2025.

45 Biographical sketch of Adella Emma Potter, by Michelle Moravec. Included in *Part III: Mainstream Suffragists—National American Woman Suffrage Association*. Alexander Street, part of Clarivate.

46 "Mrs. Adella E. Potter," *Orlando (FL) Evening Star*, November 2, 1966.

47 Janet Lindenmuth, "Ruza Wenclawska: Suffragist, Labor Organizer, Poet and Actor," https://janetlindenmuth.com/2024/10/01/ruza-wenclawska-suffragist-labor-organizer-poet-and-actor/, October 1, 2024.

48 "Miss Winslow on the Issue of Suffrage: Leading Feminist Speaker to Invade City and County Soon: To Conclude Her Campaign in City: Winds Up with Meetings in New Castle Saturday Afternoon and Night," *New Castle (PA) Herald*, August 17, 1915.

49 Janet Lindenmuth, "Ruza Wenclawska: Suffragist, Labor Organizer, Poet and Actor," *Medium*, June 23, 2024.

50 "Lucretia Longshore Blankenburg," in *Notable American Women, 1607–1950*, vol. 1, A–F, ed. Radcliffe College (Cambridge, MA: Belknap Press of Harvard University Press, 1971), 170.

51 Ancestry.com and FamilySearch online entries for Kate Chapman (1865–1937).

52 Henrietta Louise Krone, "Dauntless Women: The Story of the Woman Suffrage Movement in Pennsylvania, 1910–20" (PhD diss., University of Pennsylvania, 1946), 72.

53 "Biographical Sketch of Kate A. R. Chapman," by Christina Larocco. Included in *Part III: Mainstream Suffragists—National American Woman Suffrage Association*. Alexander Street, part of Clarivate.

54 "Women Gather in Quaker City to Hear Peals of Liberty Bell: Mrs. Maxwell Chapman to Be Present When Famous Bell Is Rung for First Time," *Tribune* (Scranton, PA), September 24, 1920.

55 "Mrs. Kate Chapman, Suffrage and Civic Leader, Dies Here: Was First Woman to Seek Elective Office," *Tribune* (Scranton, PA), July 10, 1937.

56 "When the Women's Suffrage Bell Toured the Valley," *Valley Girl Views*, Heather Truckenmiller's blog about the Central Susquehanna Valley, August 17, 2020.

57 "Biographical Sketch of Mary Ella Bakewell," by Beyer. Included in *Part III: Mainstream Suffragists—National American Woman Suffrage Association*. Alexander Street, part of Clarivate.

58 *Stories for Kindergartners and Kindchen* (Pittsburgh: Pittsburgh Printing, 1901) and *True Fairy Stories* (New York: American Book Company, 1902).

59 "Gave Up Her Law Practice to Talk Socialism on the Street: Mrs. Gertrude Breslau Hunt Says It Takes Strenuous Measures to Protect Your Voice Against Cincinnati Atmosphere—Kidnapped When a Child, and Restored to Parents in a Peculiar Manner," *Cincinnati (OH) Post*, November 3, 1904.

60 "Gave Up Her Law Practice," *Cincinnati (OH) Post*, November 3, 1904.

61 "A Picture for the Democrats: It Is Offered to the County Organization by the Socialists," *Reading (PA) Times*, January 8, 1921.

62 "Gertrude Breslau Hunt," Wikipedia, last modified January 3, 2025.

63 "Suffragette Bell Ends County Tour," *York (PA) Dispatch*, October 9, 1915.

64 "Biographical Sketch of Ethel Ridgley Vorce," by Abigail M. Leedom and Liette Gidlow. Included in *Part III: Mainstream Suffragists—National American Woman Suffrage Association*. Alexander Street, part of Clarivate.

65 "Biographical Sketch of Antoinette Funk," by Andrew Daily, Eric Brooks, and Nathan Rees. Included in *Part III: Mainstream Suffragists—National American Woman Suffrage Association*. Alexander Street, part of Clarivate.

66 "Suffragists Here Over Yellow Path to Obtain Votes: Liberty Bell Center of Admiring Throng in Penn Street Parade: Women Argue Rights," *Reading (PA) Times*, October 14, 1915.

67 "Antoinette Funk," Wikipedia, last modified January 22, 2025.

68 "Woman Ardmore Postmaster," *Philadelphia Inquirer*, March 10, 1911.

69 Katie Hickey, "Mary Jenkins Ensign: The Woman Who Made News," Ardmore Project: Suburban Life in the Early 20th Century. Falvey Library. Villanova University's Digital Library. Villanova, PA.

70 "Our Special Suffrage Issue," *Ardmore Chronicle*—volume XXVI, No. 30, (Ardmore PA), May 1, 1915. Source: Historical Society of Montgomery County.

71 "Ardmore Women Greet Suffrage Liberty Bell," *Evening Public Ledger* (Philadelphia, PA), October 22, 1915.

72 *Find a Grave* database memorial page for Alice Katharine Huey Bedford (June 27, 1877–October 15, 1960). Memorial ID 60757445, citing West Laurel Hill Cemetery, Bala Cynwyd, Montgomery County, Pennsylvania.

73 "Delegates to Suffrage Convention," *Delaware County Daily Times* (Chester, PA), November 18, 1912.

74 "County Chairman of Woman Suffrage Party: Mrs. Charles E. Martin, of Wayne, Elected to Succeed Mrs. J. Claude Bedford, of Media," *Delaware County Daily Times* (Chester, PA), December 7, 1915.

75 "Suffrage Meetings," *Delaware County Times* (Chester, PA), September 18, 1915.

76 "Bell's Welcome into the County: Enthusiastic Greetings All Along the Chester and Darby Pike to This City," *Delaware County Times* (Chester, PA), October 26, 1915.

77 "Bell's Tour in the County: Boroughs and Towns Give Emblem of Liberty an Enthusiastic Reception," *Delaware County Times* (Chester, PA), October 28, 1915.

78 "Mrs. J. Bedford Dies at Age 83 in Media Home," *Philadelphia Inquirer*, October 16, 1960.

79 "The Women Rest Their Case," *Pittston (PA) Gazette*, November 1, 1915.

80 Henrietta Louise Krone, "Dauntless Women: The Story of the Woman Suffrage Movement in Pennsylvania, 1910–20" (PhD diss., University of Pennsylvania, 1946), 114–24.

81 "Women Thank the Voters of Chester County: Say Men Emphatically Registered Their Trust in Opposite Sex Having the Ballot," *Daily Local News* (West Chester, PA), November 24, 1915.

82 Pennsylvania was not the only state where men voted on women's suffrage amendments in 1915. New York and Massachusetts held referendums on November 2, while New Jersey's referendum took place on October 19. In all four states, the majority of men voted to deny women the right to vote.

PART THREE
After the Tour

1 Lucas Bensley, "Suffer Not the Rain: The 1916 Suffrage Parade in Chicago," published on March 1, 2020, on Suffrage 2020 Illinois, a blog of the Evanston History Center. Online at https://suffrage2020illinois.org/2020/03/01/suffer-not-the-rain-the–16-suffrage-parade-in-chicago/.

2 Amy Ensley, "Hannah J. Patterson: Feminist Trailblazer: Suffrage Plank Included in Republican and Democratic Platforms," online exhibit, Hankey Center, Wilson College, 2021. Online at https://exhibits.wilson.edu/exhibits/show/hannah-j-patterson-feminist/secretary-of-the-national-amer

3 "Suffragists Elated Over Their Work at Convention," *Daily Herald* (Monongahela, PA), June 15, 1916.

4 "Suffragists Open Fall Campaign: They Choose Wednesday As Conference Day and Hope for Workers: Party Women Active in Canning, Gardening and Red Cross Work. May Take Interest in County Fair and Primary Elections," *Daily Local News* (West Chester, PA), August 16, 1917.

5 "Liberty Bell for Senators from Women: Individual Photos Sent to Recall Constantly Plea of Suffragists," *Washington Herald* (Washington, DC), March 4, 1918.

6 "Women to March Today Behind the Liberty Bell," *Washington Post* (Washington, DC), April 26, 1918.

7 "Liberty Loan Army Trains for Drive," *Philadelphia Inquirer*, September 24, 1918.

8 "Women Prepare for the Loan March: Bell Built for Suffragists Reconsecrated and Will Appear on Float," *Evening Public Ledger* (Philadelphia), September 28, 1918.

9 "Woman's Suffrage Passes House, 153 to 44; This State Seventh to Ratify," *Evening News* (Harrisburg, PA), June 24, 1919.

10 "Pennsylvania Falls in Line for Suffrage; Vote of House Completes Ratification: Mrs. Miller Speaks," *Pittsburgh Post-Gazette*, June 25, 1919.

11 "Mother's Plea Saved Vote for Sex: Harry T. Burn of Niota, Lauded as Man Who Turned the Tide," *Journal and Tribune* (Knoxville, TN), August 22, 1920.

12 "Suffrage Bell to Break Silence: First Clang from Duplicate of Famous Relic to Be Heard Here September 25: Plan Big Celebration," *Evening Public Ledger* (Philadelphia, PA), September 21, 1920.

13 "Woman's Justice Bell Will Ring This Afternoon: Distinguished Gathering

Will Take Part in Independence Square Exercise: To Mark Final Victory After Years of Effort: Tributes Will Be Paid to Pioneers in Great Campaign for Suffrage," *Evening Public Ledger* (Philadelphia, PA), September 25, 1920.

14 "Justice Bell to Peal Tidings of Woman's Victory," *Evening Public Ledger* (Philadelphia, PA), September 25, 1920.

15 "'Justice Bell' Rung by Suffragists to Proclaim Victory," *Pittsburgh Post-Gazette*, September 26, 1920.

16 "Woman's Justice Bell Will Ring This Afternoon: Distinguished Gathering Will Take Part in Independence Square Exercises," *Evening Public Ledger* (Philadelphia, PA), September 25, 1920.

17 Maud Wood Park, Carrie Chapman Catt, and National American Woman Suffrage Association Collection, Front Door Lobby [S.l.: s.n., 192, 1920] Manuscript/Mixed Material. Online at https://www.loc.gov/item/93838361/.

PART FOUR
What Happened to the Justice Bell?

1 "Liberty Bell Going Through Town: Special Places Will Hold Special Celebrations Tomorrow: Malvern and Valley Forge to See Presentations of Flags and Ceremonies by Patriotic Committee," *Daily Local News* (West Chester, PA), July 3, 1923.

2 "Get Out the Vote Caravan Off Today: Celebration in Independence Square to Mark Departure of Crusaders," *Philadelphia Inquirer*, October 1, 1924.

3 "Schuylkill Women Urged to Vote at Big Meeting in County," *Pottsville (PA) Republican*, October 3, 1924.

4 "Duty of Voting Made Impressive by Vote Caravan: League of Women Voters and Others Meet Travelers, Who Speak with Local Persons: Percentages Low," *Brookville (PA) American*, October 16, 1924.

5 Katharine Wentworth Ruschenberger, *Last Will and Testament,* February 28, 1936. Courtesy of Alexandra Tatnall, great-niece of Katharine Wentworth Ruschenberger.

6 "Justice Bell Off on Anniversary Tour," *Philadelphia Inquirer*, April 25, 1995.

7 "Justice Bell Is Dedicated in Valley Forge Memorial Chapel," *Phoenixville (PA) Community Courier*, September 3, 1997.

8 "Cyclist Rings the Bell to Promote Her Passion," *Philadelphia Inquirer*, June 21, 2004.

9 Melissa Callahan "Commemorating the Justice Bell Tour," *CrossTies Newsletter*, Mid-Atlantic Regional Center for the Humanities, Rutgers University, Camden, NJ, November 5, 2015.

Image Credits

PART ONE

p. ii: Pennsylvania Woman Suffrage Association, "Assorted Handbills Supporting the 1915 Referendum Campaign," Woman's Suffrage Movement in Pennsylvania Collection, University of Pittsburgh, AIS.2021.19, Identifier 31735072991031.

p. 2: National American Woman Suffrage Association, "Flier: Votes for Women a Success The Map Proves It. [1915]," Ann Lewis Women's Suffrage Collection, https://lewissuffragecollection.omeka.net/items/show/1296.

p. 3: "Mrs. Frank M. Roessing, President of the Pennsylvania Woman Suffrage Association," *Pittsburgh Post*, November 7, 1915.

p. 7: "Women's Parade Tops Inaugural: Suffragists' Pageant on Streets of Washington Tomorrow," *Philadelphia Inquirer*, March 2, 1913.

p. 8: Kenneth Florey, *American Woman Suffrage Postcards: A Study and Catalog* (Jefferson, NC: McFarland & Company, 2015). Used with permission.

p. 8: "The Liberty Bell Float, a Striking Feature of Parade," *Brooklyn (NY) Daily Eagle*, November 2, 1913.

p. 9: Women's Suffrage Convention, Scranton, Pennsylvania, ca. 1914. General Files (Series #73m.1); MG-73, Liliane Stevens Howard Collection, Pennsylvania State Archives, Harrisburg.

p. 9: "Woman's Liberty Bell to Visit This County: On Tour of State in the Interest of Equal Rights for Women," *Brockwayville Record* (Brockway, PA), July 16, 1915.

p. 11: Photograph (cropped) courtesy of Alexandra Tatnall, great-niece of Katharine Wentworth Ruschenberger.

p. 14: Pictured: Miss Lida Stokes Adams, Mrs. George H. Robin Smith, Mrs. George A. Peirsol, Mrs. Frank M. Roessing, Mrs. George A. Dunning,

Mrs. Harry E. Con, Miss Sophia H. Dolan, Mrs. Thomas S. Kirkbride, Mrs. John Cook Hearst, Mrs. Bakewell Green, Miss Dell Hastings, Mrs. H. H. Donaldson, Mrs. Ferdinand H. Greyser, and Miss Caroline Katzenstein. Photograph from "Suffragists Leave City to See 'Justice Bell' Cast in Troy," *Evening Public Ledger* (Philadelphia, PA), March 30, 1915.

p. 14: Bain News Service Collection, Library of Congress, Prints and Photographs Division, LC-DIG-ggbain-18817.

p. 15: "Mrs. Katharine Wentworth Ruschenberger," *Delaware County Daily Times* (Chester, PA), April 1, 1915.

PART TWO

p. 18: Photograph by Oliver Hall, from Ethel Bret Harte Album, Liberty Bell Tour, 1915, MC 952, folder 1.1, Schlesinger Library, Radcliffe Institute, Harvard University, Cambridge, MA.

p. 18: Photograph by Oliver Hall, from Ethel Bret Harte Album, Liberty Bell Tour, 1915, MC 952, folder 1.1, Schlesinger Library, Radcliffe Institute, Harvard University, Cambridge, MA.

p. 24: Sara "Sallie" Corbishley, "Map of the 1915 Justice Bell tour route," 1995. Courtesy of Sara "Sallie" Corbishley, from her private papers.

p. 24: Amanda Owen, "Map of the 1915 Justice Bell tour," 2025. Reconstructed by the author based on original research; Pennsylvania counties map by suncatcherstudio.com. Used with permission.

p. 27: Amanda Owen, "Map of the 1915 Justice Bell tour," 2025. Reconstructed by the author based on original research; Pennsylvania counties map by suncatcherstudio.com. Used with permission.

p. 28: Photograph by Oliver Hall, from Women's Liberty Bell Tour of 1915 Photographs, League of Women Voters records. Call number 2095, Permanent ID 2597. Historical Society of Pennsylvania, 1915.

p. 31: *The Woman Citizen*, Vols. 1–3 (February 1912–October 1913), 13. California State Library. Publication date 1912.

p. 34: Mary M. Wolfe, Superintendent, Item 5. Lantern Slides of Laurelton State Village (Series #23.934); RG-23, Department of Human Services. Pennsylvania State Archives, Harrisburg, PA.

p. 36: "Eudora Ramsay Richardson (1891–1973)," by Andrea Ledesma, in *Dictionary of Virginia Biography*. Library of Virginia (1998–), published 2018.

p. 38: "Suffrage Head Appeals to the Women of Erie," *Erie (PA) Daily Times*, July 5, 1913.

p. 40: Kenneth Florey, *American Woman Suffrage Postcards: A Study and Catalog* (Jefferson, NC: McFarland & Company, 2015). Used with permission.

p. 40: Kenneth Florey, *American Woman Suffrage Postcards: A Study and Catalog* (Jefferson, NC: McFarland & Company, 2015). Used with permission.

p. 43: "Plan Greeting for Liberty Bell Party," *New Castle (PA) Herald*, June 30, 1915.

p. 46: Photograph titled "Council of National Defense—Miss Hannah J. Patterson, of Woman's Committee, Council of National Defense," 1917–18. National Archives and Records Administration. Wikimedia Commons.

p. 49: Photograph courtesy of Eliza Smith Brown, from her private collection.

p. 54: Photograph by Oliver Hall, from Women's Liberty Bell Tour of 1915 Photographs, League of Women Voters records. Call number 2095, Permanent ID 2597. Historical Society of Pennsylvania, 1915.

p. 58: Senior-year yearbook entry, *Vassarion*, 1913. Vassar College Libraries. From the Elizabeth McShane Hilles Papers. Schlesinger Library, Radcliffe Institute, Harvard University.

p. 61: "Works Year for Suffrage in Wis.," *Bisbee (AZ) Daily Review*, November 5, 1912, in Chronicling America: Historic American Newspapers. Library of Congress. Image provided by Arizona State Library, Archives and Public Records, Phoenix, AZ.

p. 67: "Will Parade Bell Through Streets: Local Suffragists and Municipal Band to Greet Campaign Party," *Harrisburg (PA) Daily Independent*, September 28, 1915.

p. 70: Photograph by Oliver Hall, from Women's Liberty Bell Tour of 1915 Photographs, League of Women Voters records. Call number 2095, Permanent ID 2597. Historical Society of Pennsylvania, 1915.

p. 70: Photograph by Oliver Hall, from Ethel Bret Harte Album, Liberty Bell Tour, 1915, MC 952, folder 1.1, Schlesinger Library, Radcliffe Institute, Harvard University, Cambridge, MA.

p. 76: Photograph of Alice Kiernan courtesy of the Historical and Genealogical Society of Somerset County.

p. 79: "Mrs. Susan W. Fitzgerald," ca. 1910–1915, Bain News Service, publisher. Library of Congress Prints and Photographs Division.

p. 80: Photograph by Oliver Hall, from Women's Liberty Bell Tour of 1915 Photographs, League of Women Voters records. Call number 2095, Permanent ID 2597. Historical Society of Pennsylvania, 1915.

p. 80: Photograph by Oliver Hall, from Ethel Bret Harte Album, Liberty Bell Tour, 1915, MC 952, folder 1.1, Schlesinger Library, Radcliffe Institute, Harvard University, Cambridge, MA.

p. 87: Papers of Ethel Bret Harte, Album, Liberty Bell Tour, 1915, MC 952, folder 1.1, Schlesinger Library, Radcliffe Institute, Harvard University, Cambridge, MA.

p. 88: Photograph by Oliver Hall, from Women's Liberty Bell Tour of 1915 Photographs, League of Women Voters records. Call number 2095, Permanent ID 2597. Historical Society of Pennsylvania, 1915.

p. 88: Photograph by Oliver Hall, from Ethel Bret Harte Album, Liberty Bell Tour, 1915, MC 952, folder 1.1, Schlesinger Library, Radcliffe Institute, Harvard University, Cambridge, MA.

p. 94: "Town and Country Ready for Suffrage Bell Campaigners," *Selinsgrove (PA) Times-Tribune*, September 23, 1915.

p. 96: Photograph by Oliver Hall, from Women's Liberty Bell Tour of 1915 Photographs, League of Women Voters records. Call number 2095, Permanent ID 2597. Historical Society of Pennsylvania, 1915.

p. 96: Photograph by Oliver Hall, from Ethel Bret Harte Album, Liberty Bell Tour, 1915, MC 952, folder 1.1, Schlesinger Library, Radcliffe Institute, Harvard University, Cambridge, MA.

p. 100: Photograph (cropped) originally published in *The Suffragist*, 1916–. National Woman's Party Records, Group I, Container I:158, Folder: Winslow, Rose. Library of Congress.

p. 103: Caroline Katzenstein Papers, Collection Am 8996, Historical Society of Pennsylvania.

p. 105: "Mrs. Kate Chapman, Suffrage and Civic Leader, Dies Here: Was First Woman in County's History to Seek Elective Office," *The Tribune* (Scranton, PA), July 10, 1937.

p. 108: Photograph by Oliver Hall, from Women's Liberty Bell Tour of 1915 Photographs, League of Women Voters records. Call number 2095,

Permanent ID 2597. Historical Society of Pennsylvania, 1915.

p. 112: Caroline Katzenstein Papers, Collection Am 8996, Historical Society of Pennsylvania.

p. 116: "A Word from the Self-Supporting Woman," *Socialist Spirit 2*, no. 1 (September 1902).

p. 118: Photograph by Albert Allen Line, from Line Collection, Catalog Number 00717A, Cumberland County Historical Society, Carlisle, PA.

p. 124: Photograph from "Myron B. Vorce," *Fulton County News* (McConnellsburg, PA), September 30, 1915.

p. 132: Identified suffragists in the photograph: Antoinette Funk is standing on the platform to the left. Dr. Mary Wolfe is standing on the ground on the far left. Next to her is possibly Doris Long, president of the Lebanon chapter of the Pennsylvania Woman Suffrage Association. At the center of the photo, in front of the bell, is Elizabeth McShane. Photograph courtesy of Michael Trump, from his private collection.

p. 132: Photograph by Oliver Hall, from Ethel Bret Harte Album, Liberty Bell Tour, 1915, MC 952, folder 1.1, Schlesinger Library, Radcliffe Institute, Harvard University, Cambridge, MA.

p. 136: "Mrs. Antoinette Funk," ca. 1915 Bain News Service, publisher. Library of Congress Prints and Photographs Division.

p. 135: "Bright Women Able Editors," *Philadelphia Inquirer*, October 2, 1902.

p. 147: Chester County History Center, West Chester, PA. Identifier MsColl235_001_015.

p. 150: Photograph (cropped) from *The Woman Citizen*, vol. 2, May 18, 1918.

p. 153: Map published by the Pennsylvania Men's League for Woman Suffrage. Caroline Katzenstein Papers, Collection Am 8996, Historical Society of Pennsylvania.

PART THREE

p. 158: Photograph by Harris & Ewing, from Woman Suffrage: Liberty Bell for Suffrage (Washington, DC: 1916). Harris & Ewing Photograph Collection, Library of Congress, Prints and Photographs Division, Washington, DC. Call Number LC-H261-6148. Digital ID: hec.06745.

p. 166: Photograph courtesy of the Special Collections Research Center, Temple University Libraries, Philadelphia, PA.

PART FOUR

P. 172: "To House 'Justice Bell': Suffrage Leaders Plan Tower for Independence Square," *Philadelphia Inquirer*, March 3, 1921.

p. 172: "Big Suffrage Bell Fallen From Grace: Woman's Symbol of Right to Vote Rests in City Slaughter House," *Philadelphia Inquirer*, May 26, 1921.

p. 172: "Justice Bell Seeks Shrine," *Philadelphia Inquirer*, June 23, 1938.

p. 180: Photograph of the Justice Bell at Washington Memorial Chapel by Amanda Owen, August 29, 2023.

Bring the Justice Bell Story to Your Community

Host a Screening or Book Event

Amanda Owen offers virtual and in-person presentations, book signings, and screenings of the PBS-aired documentary *Finding Justice: The Untold Story of Women's Fight for the Vote*—a companion to *The Justice Bell: Tracing the Journey of a Forgotten Symbol*. Events can be tailored for schools, libraries, museums, civic groups, book clubs, and conferences.

> "Amanda does not merely teach history—she brings it to life, inspiring young women to see themselves as changemakers." —Kim A. Yacoubian, Executive Director, Girls Spark

> "*Finding Justice* is not only a film that inspires and empowers—it's a testament to the courage and resilience of the women who helped lead the charge for suffrage." —Jennifer Herrera, Vice President of External Affairs, National Women's History Museum

Book Clubs and Classroom Use

Reading guides and educational materials are available to support discussion and learning. Explore how the Justice Bell connects to broader themes of women's rights, civic engagement, and American history.

Suggested Uses

- Women's History Month events
- Civic engagement and voter registration initiatives
- Museum exhibitions or local history programs
- University or high school coursework in history or gender studies

Signed Copies

Signed copies are available upon request for events, speaking engagements, and educational use.

Contact & More Information

To schedule a presentation or learn more about the Justice Bell Foundation's work, visit: www.justicebell.org. Learn about the Justice Bell archive at Montgomery County Community College in Blue Bell, Pennsylvania at mc3.edu/JusticeBell

About the Author

Amanda Owen is a writer, independent historian, filmmaker, and the cofounder and executive director of the Justice Bell Foundation (JBF), a nonprofit dedicated to reclaiming women's history and promoting voter participation. On behalf of the foundation, she wrote and directed *Finding Justice: The Untold Story of Women's Fight for the Vote*, a documentary that premiered at the National Women's History Museum and aired on PBS stations. In partnership with the Pennsylvania Academy of the Fine Arts, the JBF commissioned a traveling replica of the Justice Bell and developed a school program introducing children to the history of the women's suffrage movement. Her book, *The Justice Bell: Tracing the Journey of a Forgotten Symbol*, presents the first full account of the Justice Bell's journey. She is also the author of *The Power of Receiving* and *Born to Receive*, both published by Penguin Random House.

Index

www.ingramcontent.com/pod-product-compliance
Lightning Source LLC
LaVergne TN
LVHW010651110826
845149LV00014B/3042

* 9 7 8 0 9 8 4 8 2 0 9 1 7 *